PINEWOOD DERBY FAST AND FURIOUS
SPEED SECRETS

Special thanks to our test cutters, Rolf Beuttenmuller and Leldon Maxcy.

©2017 by Fox Chapel Publishing Company, Inc., East Petersburg, PA.

ISBN 978-1-56523-904-3

To learn more about the other great books from Fox Chapel Publishing,
or to find a retailer near you, call toll-free 800-457-9112
or visit us at www.FoxChapelPublishing.com.

Note to Authors: We are always looking for talented authors to write new books. Please send a brief letter describing your idea to Acquisitions Editor, 1970 Broad Street, East Petersburg, PA 17520.

Printed in the United States of America
First printing

PINEWOOD DERBY *FAST AND FURIOUS* *SPEED SECRETS*

Tips & Tricks for Building Winning Cars

By David Meade, Troy Thorne, Jon Deck,
and Other Derby Experts

Fox Chapel
PUBLISHING

CONTENTS

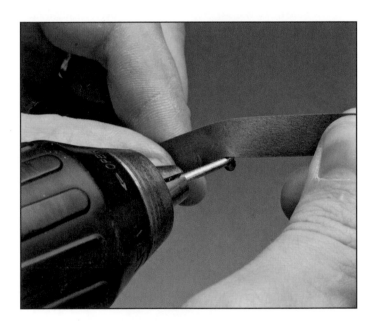

PINEWOOD DERBY... MORE THAN JUST A CAR!

By Joe Gargiulo of Pinewood Pro

I remember the excitement of building a Pinewood Derby car with my dad when I was a young Cub Scout. Dad listened carefully to my wild ideas and then helped me build the car of my dreams. It seemed to take forever to shape, sand, and prep my car, but I didn't mind at all. This was "Dad time," and since there were four of us kids, "Dad time" was hard to come by. We barely finished the car the night before the race. I named it the *Flying Blue Marlin*, after my favorite fish.

On race day I was an excited little boy, even though, race after race, my car barely made it to the bottom of the track. I was disappointed, but I was still proud of my cool little car. I treasured that car and the time spent with my dad. I lost my dad when I was 22, so those memories are priceless.

I lost track of my car over the years and always thought it had been thrown away. Forty years later, while cleaning out my parents' house, I was amazed to find it in the attic on top of a heap of things and in perfect condition, as if my father had placed it there for me to find. It was a surreal moment.

When my son came along, I got to relive my cherished childhood Pinewood Derby experiences with him. (Only now I had an engineering degree under my belt so we were able to skip some of the disappointment.) I treasured the time with Steven, just as I had the time with my dad so many years ago.

Having Fun Together ... as a Team

Pinewood Derby racing was invented by Don Murphy to "foster a closer parent-child relationship." That makes the two of you a team. So, who does what? Your child should do as many age-appropriate things as he safely can. Encourage him to be creative selecting a car design, and then build the car according to his ideas. Every child can decide a color scheme, paint and decorate the car, and give the car a name.

As children get older, they can use a coping saw and wood rasp, and sand the car under supervision. The more they do, the more they will feel like it is their car.

Dad, Mom, or a grandparent should help plan the project (hint: start early), provide the tools and materials, use power tools as needed, and help with intricate tasks that require more dexterity. While building the car together, take time to teach your child to be creative, to use tools safely, and to show good sportsmanship. Most importantly, remind him to have fun, even when he makes a cutting mistake, spills paint, or his car doesn't win every heat.

I treasure the memories of building this car with my dad (above) and of helping my son when he was a Scout (left).

Teaching the Speed Secrets

This book will help you build a fast Pinewood Derby car. Take the time to teach your child not just the speed techniques but also the principles behind them. Explain that among the many factors that contribute to making a fast car, you need to minimize friction, set the optimal center of gravity, and maximize the weight so the car will speed to the finish line. Explain how wheel alignment, wheel preparation, and axle preparation make the car faster. In a fun way, you are essentially teaching the physics of motion and fundamentals of STEM (science, technology, engineering, math). The Pinewood Derby is a microcosm of a complete engineering project cycle—creative design, hard work, engineering the car for speed, testing, and rework—all within a fixed time frame where the deadline can't be moved.

So work hard, have fun, and encourage your child to be proud of his car. Above all, he will remember the closeness and time spent building a car together.

Oh, and that cool little car that I built with my dad 50 years ago? I keep it on my desk so I never lose it again.

The idea of making your own race car is exciting—but where do you start? Turn the page to learn the history of the Derby and see some winning designs from fellow Cub Scouts across the country. You'll also find an overview of the official rules and some local variations, safety equipment and guidelines, and a few suggestions for a successful race day. Review this section to see what's possible, and then keep reading to find out how to make it happen!

1 2
3 4
5 6
7 8
9 0

A CUB SCOUT/PARENT PROJECT
KIT NO. 17006

OFFICIAL GRAND P

The Pinewood Derby is open to all Cub Scouts. Ca
guidance. Any technical assistance should be fully ex
knowledge on future projects. Because it is difficult to e
some Packs have a separate Pinewood Derby Race for ad

IMPORTANT: The Race Committee should decide on rules an
distributed to all participants at least two weeks before the race.

CAR SPECIFICATIONS:
- Width – 2 3/4" • Length – 7" • Weight –
- Width between wheels – 1 3/4"
- Bottom clearance between car and track – 3/

washers and bushings are prohibited. The car shall not ride on springs.
Pinewood Derby wheels and axles are permitted. Only dry lubricant is permitted
eel and driver are permissible as long as these details do not exceed the maximum
ecifications. The car must be free-wheeling, with no starting devices. Each car
will be informed of the reason for failure, and will be given time within the offi
make the adjustment. After final approval, cars will not be reinspected un
in a race.

each is at a perfect 90-degree angle to the car be
the other, causing it to rub up against the side
gles by using a square, a protractor, or
de to redress the slots. Use the er

Only offici
Pe
br

Choo ur favorite design, then mark the
gently drive the axles into the grooves wil
pliers, remove axles by pulling and tur
of the cutting can be done with a
and scoops should be added no
built into the car.
NOTE: If the car design
the body remains 1 3/

PAINTING
Apply se
two co

HISTORY OF THE PINEWOOD DERBY

The moment the first group of miniature cars started down the 32-foot race ramp with the battery-run finish line made from doorbells, the Pinewood Derby enjoyed instant success.

The creation of a California Cubmaster, Donald Murphy, the Derby arose from his search for an activity that he and his 10-year-old son could work on together. Murphy, an art director, was inspired by his employer, North American Aviation, which sponsored Soap Box Derby races, as well as by his own childhood experiences.

"I'd made models of airplanes, cars, boats, and any number of other structures and remembered the pleasure I got out of doing it," Murphy told *Scouting* magazine in November 1999. "I also wanted to devise a wholesome, constructive activity that would foster a closer father-son relationship and promote craftsmanship and good sportsmanship through competition."

FOR 60 YEARS, MILLIONS OF KIDS HAVE LEARNED SPORTSMANSHIP AND WOODWORKING BY BUILDING MINIATURE CARS

Murphy presented his idea for carving and racing miniature cars to Cub Scout Pack 280C of Manhattan Beach, Calif. The pack heartily endorsed the project. Murphy then designed a gravity-propelled car that could be carved out of soft pine and wrote the rules for racing the miniature vehicles. Those rules stated, "The Derby is run in heats on a two- to four-lane track. Two to four cars starting from a standstill will run self-propelled down an inclined track to the finish line. Cars are guided by a raised spacer on the track between the wheels."

The first Pinewood Derby was held on May 15, 1953, at the pack's newly constructed Scout House in Manhattan Beach. The Management Club at North American Aviation sponsored the event. Contestants from the 55-member Cub Scout pack, using kits consisting of a block of pine, two wooden axles, four nails, and four wheels, raced in three classes: Class A, for 10-year-olds; Class B, for nine-year-olds; and Class C, for eight-year-olds.

The following year, a local newspaper and the Los Angeles City Recreation and Parks Department sponsored a citywide Pinewood Derby and the national office of the Boy Scouts of America® adopted the program for Cub Scout packs nationwide.

The first Pinewood Derby was held in Manhattan Beach, Calif., in 1953. The race became a nationwide program the following year.

More than 60 years after the running of the first Pinewood Derby, the event continues to be immensely popular not only among Cub Scouts® (more than 100 million of whom have participated in the Derby to date), but with members of other youth groups as well. The program has been adopted by the Girl Scouts®, Awana® Clubs International (as the Awana Grand Prix), Scouts Canada (as the Kub Kar Rally), the Christian Service Brigade® (as the Shape N Race Derby), the Royal Rangers®, the YMCA Adventure Guides®, and the Woodcar Independent Racing League (WIRL). It also has spawned related events, such as the Raingutter Regatta®, which uses boats instead of cars, and the Space Derby®, which uses rockets.

The Pinewood Derby has also spawned a whole genre of products and services for car builders and racers.

When the Pinewood Derby observed its fiftieth birthday in 2003, Murphy, then 83 years old, was honored with a proclamation from the president of the United States. He also received commendations from the national director of Cub Scouting, the governor of California, both of California's U.S. senators, and the mayor of Los Angeles. In Manhattan Beach, the Derby's birthplace, Pack 713, a direct descendant of Pack 280C, hosted a commemoration for the city's Cub Scouts, staging several races with retro 1953 cars in the same Scout House that was the site of the first Derby.

Because of Don Murphy, Father of the Pinewood Derby, generations of parents and children have built strong relationships as they develop valuable skills.

Murphy's legacy lives on.

WORLD CHAMPIONSHIP

For six hours on a summer Saturday, Cub Scouts ruled New York City's Times Square. More than 250 Cub Scouts and their families from across the country crowded bleachers set up in the midst of the lights and electronic billboards and raced their handmade wooden cars in the second annual Pinewood Derby World Championship.

To qualify for the race, each Scout had to place first, second, or third in his age division at a District or Council championship race and be a registered Scout. Because various Councils have adopted different rules over the years, the World Championship has two divisions: the Stock Car Series and the Pro Stock Series. All of the cars must be made from the official kit, but Stock Cars follow the strictest rules and are the least modified, while Pro Stock cars can use many of the tips and tricks developed by adult racers.

In both divisions, the cars are breathtakingly fast. Although the entire event lasted six hours, each race took an average of just three seconds. Some cars were traveling more than 10 miles per hour down the aluminum track. The World Championship car in the Pro Stock division had a winning time of 2.9754 seconds, while the winner of the Stock Car Series clocked 3.0188 seconds.

So, how did they build such fast cars? Taylor D. of the Black Swamp Area Council (Ohio), the 11-year-old winner of the Stock Car Series, worked with his dad, Jason, to build his racer. They called the car "Last Chance" because it was

Taylor's last year of eligibility for the race. Taking more than two months to build their car, the team measured and considered everything from the dryness of the wood to the weights.

Six-year-old JJ H. of the Cradle of Liberty Council in Pennsylvania, the Pro Stock Series winner, may be too young to use power tools, but he understands the physics of Derby cars and worked closely with his grandfather, Joe Brewster, to build his winning car. Joe said, "When you start building a car for speed, you have to follow the universal laws on physics. The more weight you have further back in the car, the faster the car is going to be." He also mentioned experimenting with several car designs, smoothing the wheels, axles, and car body, and using a test track to tune the car's alignment. Joe added, "We didn't expect to win anything up there. We just wanted to do our best, and it turned out we did really well."

In the end, nearly 40 trophies were awarded for winners in each age division as well as specialty categories like Most Patriotic and Best Scout Theme. However, many of the Cub Scouts and their families considered themselves winners just for taking part in the event. As Joe Brewster said, "We wanted to take JJ there more for the totality of the event, not just to race cars, but for the experience of being in New York City. The event as a whole was a real prize. You don't get a bigger venue than Times Square."

WHAT DOES IT TAKE TO BE WORLD CHAMP?

Above: Taylor D. won the Stock Car Series with a time of 3.0188 seconds. Right: JJ H. won the Pro Stock Series with a time of 2.9754 seconds.

The World Championship is hosted by the Greater New York Councils of the Boy Scouts of America. To see videos and additional photos, and for news of future events, visit www.bsa-gnyc.org/championshippinewood.

BE TRUSTWORTHY

KNOW AND FOLLOW THE RULES FOR YOUR LOCAL PINEWOOD DERBY

As you gather the tools and materials to build a car, review the official and local Pinewood Derby rules and the Official Grand Prix Pinewood Derby® car specifications. If you don't have a copy of your local rules, ask the race committee for one. Then, abide by all of the rules. Remember the principle from the Boy Scout Law: a Scout is trustworthy. If you find a design or speed tip that doesn't fit within your local Derby's rules, don't use it. If you are unsure whether something is legal, check with your local race organizer before you build the car.

The suggested rules and specifications of the Official Grand Prix Pinewood Derby® Kit are provided for reference only. Request a list of your local pack's or district's rules from your Derby organizer.

Official Size Limitations

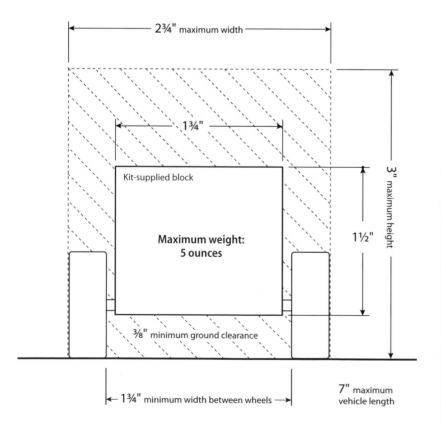

Official Grand Prix Pinewood Derby® Rules

1. Wheel bearings, washers, and bushings are prohibited.
2. The car shall not ride on springs.
3. Only official Cub Scout Grand Prix Pinewood Derby wheels and axles are permitted.
4. Only dry lubricant is permitted.
5. Details, such as steering wheel and driver, are permissible as long as these details do not exceed the maximum length, width, and weight specifications.
6. The car must be free-wheeling, with no starting devices.
7. Each car must pass inspection by the official inspection committee before it may compete. If, at registration, a car does not pass inspection, the owner will be informed of the reason for failure and will be given time within the official weigh-in time period to make the adjustment. After approval, cars will not be reinspected unless the car is damaged in handling or in a race.

Source: Boy Scouts of America Official
Grand Prix Pinewood Derby® Kit.

Rule Variations

It is important to understand the connection between local rules and the tips and instructions in this book. This survey of rules from Scouting councils across the country will help you interpret the rules and includes suggestions for avoiding illegal modifications.

General:

• Use of the new Official BSA precut (contoured) body kits, although not illegal, is strongly discouraged because it does not align with the goals of this event.
(Jersey Shore Council, N.J.)

If your race forbids kits but you don't own tools, another adult in the pack might be able to help your child cut a simple car design. The most basic cars need only a straight saw (see page 54).

• The BSA National Supply Pinewood Derby Car, part #17006, must be used. (Michigan Crossroads Council, MI)

This implies that you cannot use lumber different from that supplied in the kit. In this case, avoid a specialty car design, like the Charger on page 81, but the designs on pages 60–80 are OK.

• The Scout is to have the personal satisfaction of building his own car from the materials provided in the kit, with the guidance and assistance of an adult.
(Lincoln Heritage Council, KY)

Adults, let the kids design and build their cars to the best of their ability and within the limits of safety.

Car Design:

• Front nose of car must not contain a notch, which will embed the racing peg. If a car's front nose is deemed to have an unfair advantage due to notching or hollowing, it will be run backwards at the discretion of the race officials.
(Indian Waters Council, S.C.)

• The front edge of the car must be no more than 1 inch above the wheel lane of the track and be at least ½ inch wide at the center of the car. No narrow pointed front ends.
(Northern Star Council, MN)

Cars must be designed to rest securely against—and completely behind—the starting pin and be easy for race officials to place on the track. See page 31.

• To prevent the possibility of objects coming off the car, weights or objects must be firmly glued, taped, or otherwise attached or affixed to the finished car. Hot glue is not reliable and should not be used. (Makahiki Council, HI)

Most rules (and common sense) state that any additions must be firmly attached to the car. In addition, moving parts are frequently prohibited, especially if they might add propulsion.

• Wheels cannot extend in front or rear of the body of the car. (Central North Carolina Council, N.C.)

• Axles and axle slots cannot be moved or modified in any way and must be used. (Gulf Stream Council, FL)

Extending the wheelbase (page 30) can shift the weight toward the rear and make your car faster, but make sure it's legal.

Axles:

• Axle shafts must be from the Official BSA Pinewood Derby Kit and may only have the burrs and ridges smoothed and polished. No slotted axles are allowed. The axle head must not be modified by bending or size reduction.
(Narragansett Council, R.I.)

• Axles may be filed, polished, or grooved—as long as BSA axles from the official car kit are used and the work is done by the Scout and/or his parent/guardian. You cannot bend axles. (Greater Alabama Council, AL)

If bending the axles is prohibited, install the axles as straight as possible and align the car as shown on pages 49–50.

Wheels:

• The car should be built with the intention that all four wheels are touching the racing surface. (Glacier's Edge Council, WI)

• Three of the wheels must be touching the track surface at all times. (Grand Canyon Council, AZ)

Raising one wheel (Step B on page 50) removes friction, but it can also break the rules. Align the wheel straight instead.

• The molding seam on the wheel's tread may be removed with a light hand sanding. No other wheel changes (beveling, tapering, thin sanding, wafering, lathe turning, etc.) are allowed. Sanding a wheel spun on a mandrel is not permitted, as this alters the entire wheel, not just the mold seam. The width of the wheels where they touch the track must be at least ¼ inch and flat. (Mohegan Council, MA)

• All lettering/numbering, both inside and outside, must remain visible. The fluting and other BSA markings on the outside wheel area must remain visible. Outer wheel surface may be lightly sanded, shaved or polished to remove surface imperfections, mold casting burrs, and off-center wheel bores. ... Coning the hubs and truing the inside tread edge is allowed. (Nashua Valley Council, MA)

• The portion of the wheel hub that rubs against the car body may only be polished to remove castings. No other modifications to the hub are allowable. The portion of the hub that rubs against the car body may not be rolled or beveled in any way and shall remain flat. (Pine Tree Council, ME)

As these three examples show, rules about wheel preparation vary widely. Simply skip any preparation steps, like wheel sanding (page 40) and hub coning (page 39), disallowed by your rules and focus on lubricating the wheels thoroughly (pages 40–44).

Most Scout rules disallow changing the weight or shape of the wheels (so-called V or H profiles), so we have not included those techniques in this book.

BE SAFE

PREVENT INJURIES AND DELAYS—MAKE SAFETY YOUR TOP PRIORITY

Safety Glasses

Eye protection should wrap around and protect the front and sides of the child's eyes. Put them on every time you enter the shop.

As you and your child prepare to make a Pinewood Derby car, keep the following safety points in mind.

- **Start with a clean work space.** Check for adequate lighting and ventilation. Clean up after working on the car so you can get started quickly the next time.

- **Put on safety glasses** as soon as you enter the shop. Put on additional safety gear as needed.

- **Supervise your child when using power tools.** An innocent slip can result in an injury. Even if no one gets hurt, a misstep with a power tool can slow down the building process and maybe even the car.

- **Follow the manufacturer's instructions.** Tools and other products are made to get things done fast, and the manufacturers know the best way to use them.

- **Use saws safely.** Power saws will speed up your build, but they can be dangerous if used improperly. Cut in a slow, deliberate manner. Do not force wood through the saw. Make sure the sawing area is clean. Always wear safety glasses and a dust mask when cutting.

- **Work in a well-ventilated area.** Some products, such as wood filler, glue, spray paints, and finishes, release fumes. Use them in a well-ventilated area. Avoid contact with eyes and skin by wearing gloves and safety glasses.

- **Never melt or sand lead.** Any time you melt or sand lead, you create lead fumes or dust, which are poisonous. Tungsten weights are easier to use and help you get a fast car quickly. If you choose to use lead, it should be handled only by adults taking appropriate safety precautions.

Wear dust masks to protect against harmful fumes and airborne dust or particles when sanding, applying graphite, and spray painting.

Dust Masks

For safety, wear latex or nitrile gloves when working with glues, paints, and lead.

Gloves

Wear ear protection whenever you run power equipment. Find it in the lawncare or safety section of most home centers.

Ear Protection

BE READY

The key to a successful Pinewood Derby is to show good sportsmanship and have fun.

BE PREPARED FOR THE BIG DAY

You and your child will put a lot of time and work into creating your unique Pinewood Derby car. You'll learn new skills and share some frustrating moments. These tips will help your effort pay off with a fun and, we hope, successful day at the Derby!

Practice the Weigh-In

At many Pinewood Derby weigh-ins, you will see parents lining up to place their child's car on the scale. Instead, allow your child to weigh the car. Practice at home—put the scale on the table and let your child carefully place the car on the scale, upside down so it won't roll off. Then, have him practice putting small weights (split shot, tiny screws, or bits of tungsten putty) on the scale until it reads 5.0 ounces. When you go to the weigh-in, your child will know exactly what to do and how to do it.

Adjust the Weight

You should know from your previous work on the car, as well as the practice weigh-ins, how much the car weighs. Aim for the car to be slightly under weight, about 4.95 ounces, to allow for variances in the scales. You can easily add weight at the event, but removing it is difficult and risks ruining the alignment or lubrication.

To add weight, use small weights such as split shot, tiny screws, or bits of tungsten putty. Once your child determines the proper amount at weigh-in, place the weights or press the putty into the previously drilled extra hole in the bottom of the car (see page 34 or 57). The putty will stick; use quick-drying CA glue to secure weights. If you use lead putty, be sure to follow proper safety precautions and wash your hands afterward.

Have Fun!

Remember, the most important goal of the Pinewood Derby is to have fun! Have fun by being safe, being honest, and showing good sportsmanship. Even though we have spent a lot of time talking about principles that will help you win the Pinewood Derby, your Derby experience is only a success if you enjoy the ride.

Have your child practice placing the car upside down on a scale and adding weights until the scale reads 5.0 ounces.

Pinewood Derby Car First Aid Kit

Be prepared for anything that might happen on race day with this handy first aid kit:

- Cyanoacrylate glue (CA glue, such as Super Glue®)
- Tungsten putty or extra weights
- Extra graphite lube
- Black electrical tape
- Pliers
- Hot glue gun
- Drill and bit to remove weight if needed

You do not need a shop full of tools to make a Pinewood Derby car. The goal of the event is to show your youngster how to use woodworking tools correctly and safely. It also gives you the opportunity to spend quality time with your child.

To make a car body, you really just need to be able to cut and smooth the block.

ALL ABOUT TOOLS

Check out the essential tools to make a Derby car, and then explore some that will speed up your build ... and your car.

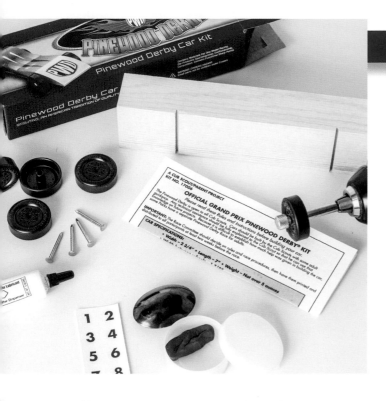

THE ESSENTIALS

Every Pinewood Derby car starts with a car kit, and needs weights and lubricant to be competitive. The kit and lubricant are available at your local craft and Scout stores; you may have to order the weights online.

• Official BSA Pinewood Derby Kit: Includes a block of wood with precut axle slots, four axles (nails), and four plastic wheels. Save the box; you'll need it to make a wheel spacer.
• Tungsten weights: Although other types of weights are available, tungsten is the best for getting the most weight exactly where you need it to be. See pages 32–34 for a detailed discussion of weights.
• Dry graphite lubricant: Dry lubricant is the only type allowed by the official Derby rules (see page 12).
• Wheel mandrel: Use to hold wheels while you work on them. See page 40. We haven't found a homemade solution that works as well.

GENERAL SUPPLIES

• Pencil
• Ruler
• Scissors
• Blue painter's tape
• Clamps
• Paper towels
• Soft rags
• Safety equipment: Goggles, mask, and gloves. See page 14 for details.
• Digital scale: The car needs to weigh close to, but not more than, 5.0 ounces.

FINDING A SCALE **TIP**
If you don't own a scale, ask if the pack will make the official scale available before the race, or the post office will often either have a scale available or weigh a car for you if asked.

You'll need a few supplies to turn the block of wood into a racer. You should be able to find most of these items around the house or at a home improvement center for minimal cost.

Push saw

Pull saw

Coping saw

Cutting

- Hand saw: Use to make long straight cuts.
  TIP: Most hand saws cut on the push stroke. It's often easier for youngsters to use a pull saw, which can be found in most home improvement stores.
- Coping saw: Use to make curved and/or inside cuts. To make inside cuts, drill a blade-entry hole, remove the blade from the frame, feed the blade through the hole, reassemble the blade with the frame, and make the cut.
  TIP: Orient a new blade so the saw cuts on the pull stroke.

Shaping

- Sandpaper: Use three grits of regular sandpaper, such as 100, 150, and 220 to roughly sand and then smooth your car. Use three grits of wet/dry sandpaper, such as 400, 600, and 1000 grit, to polish the axles and smooth the wheels.

Sandpaper

Painting & Decorating

See pages 22–28 for decorating options and supply lists.

- Newspaper, cardboard, tarp, or disposable plastic tablecloth: Protect your workspace from paint, glue, and tool mishaps.

Pipe cleaners

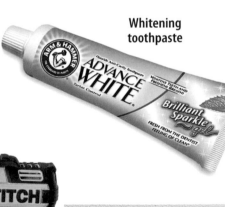

Whitening toothpaste

Polishing & Lubricating

- Pipe cleaners: Look for thick, soft cotton pipe cleaners at a tobacco or craft store. Avoid stiff, bristly types. See page 41 for details.
- Whitening toothpaste: You'll need paste, not gel. See page 41.
- Power drill: You will use it to hold the axles and wheel mandrel while you shape and polish them. See page 36.
- Homemade sanding sticks: Use to remove the burrs on the axles. Also helpful for sanding curves and inside cuts in the car body.
  TIP: To make sanding sticks, glue sandpaper to craft sticks and trim the edges with scissors. Make one stick per grit and write the grit number on the handle.

Drill

Sanding sticks

Assembling

- Sharpie marker: To insert axles. See page 48.
- Cyanoacrylate (CA) glue, such as like Krazy Glue® or Super Glue®
- Wood putty: Optional, to fill holes. See page 35. *TIP: Standard wood-matching fillers are slow-drying and brittle. Instead, use fast-drying fillers.*
- Homemade wheel spacer: Use the cardboard car kit box and tape to make a spacer, which ensures the wheels are evenly spaced when installed. See page 48.

Fast-dry filler

Glue

Wheel spacer

TIME SAVERS

A few power tools and commercial supplies can make the car-building process faster and easier. However, since most children should not handle such tools, you'll need to balance the need for speed with the pleasure of allowing your child to build the car himself.

Cutting

If you use power saws, provide a secure platform that's a safe distance away so your child can watch you cut and see how the saw works.

- Scroll saw: Scroll saws can cut very tight curves, which can be helpful when making a more complex car design. However, the wood must be less than 2 ½" thick.
- Band saw: Use a benchtop band saw with a fine ⅛"-wide blade to cut cars from thicker wood.

Scroll saw

Band saw

Shaping

- Rotary tool and bits: A rotary tool, such as a Dremel, with a variety of bits will help you shape a car quickly. The optional Flex Shaft hand piece gives you better control. Always clamp the workpiece to the table before shaping it. Suggested bits: small cylinder-shaped high-speed steel cutter; cone-shaped high-speed steel cutter; two sizes of sanding drums with an assortment of sanding drums. *TIP: When you use a bit for the first time, practice on a scrap piece of wood to get a feel for the tool before you use it on the project.*
- Power sander: Random orbital and vibrating pad sanders can be used to quickly smooth flat or convex surfaces.
- Files and rasps: The round and half-round profiles allow you to shape curved areas that your homemade sanding sticks cannot.

Rotary tool

Power sanders

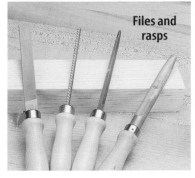

Files and rasps

Polishing & Lubricating

- Triangular file: Use instead of homemade sanding sticks to remove burrs from axles.
- Drill press: A steadier way to hold wheels and axles. With the addition of sanding drums, you can also use a drill press to shape and smooth the car.

Triangular file

Drill press

Assembling

- Wheel spacer: Set the proper distance between the wheel hub and the body quickly and easily. See page 48.

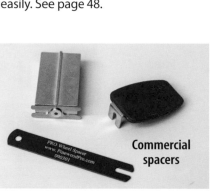

Commercial spacers

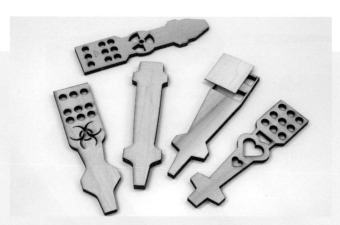

Ultimate Time Saver

If you're really pressed for time, or you don't have access to any tools, you can purchase a precut car. They are widely available in craft stores and online. Be sure to check your pack's rules and buy a car that abides by them; some precut cars are intended for adult races that have more liberal rules. You will still need to add weights, tune the wheels and axles, paint, and assemble the car.

Note: Although completely premade cars are available, we strongly discourage buying them. The purpose of the event is to practice woodworking, learn a bit of physics, and spend time together. Buying a car does not fulfill those goals.

Several companies have designed tools that will both speed the car-building process and help you refine the car to achieve premium results. Many of these tools are available only online. See the Resources on page 94 for contact information.

Cutting

- Hole driller and body tool: If you cut a car from a block of wood or choose to change the wheel spacing, you'll need to drill new axle holes. If you don't have a drill press, it will be a challenge. These tools help you drill axle holes that are perpendicular to the block. Newer models also let you drill the holes at precise angles for advanced speed techniques. (See page 46.)

Polishing & Lubricating

- Axle press: Not every axle comes out of the box perfectly straight. Pop the axle in an axle press, hit it with a hammer, and it produces a straight axle. (See page 35.)
- Hub tool: Makes it easy to clear out the wheel bore and make sure it's perpendicular to the wheel hub. (See page 39.)
- Wheel shaver: Use the shaver with a hub tool to shave wheels until they are perfectly round. The system is faster and more reliable than sanding the wheel round. (See page 39.)
- Bore polisher and polishing compounds: Use fine grits of abrasive to polish the bore better than with toothpaste. (See page 42.)

Assembling

- Center of gravity stand: A properly weighted car is literally well balanced. Use a ruler or the simpler Center of Gravity Stand to ensure the weights are right. (See page 34.)
- Axle bending tools: For some advanced speed techniques, you need to bend axles precisely; these tools help you achive the correct angles. See pages 47-51 for more information on Rail Riding and bending axles. *Note: Check your pack's rules before bending the axles.*
- Specialty weights: In addition to tungesten cubes, putty, and cylinders, you can find weights that straddle the axle slots, canopies, or other decorations to attach to the top of your racer.

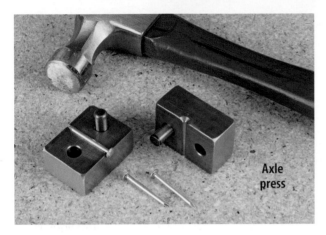

Pro body axle driller

Axle press

Specialty weights

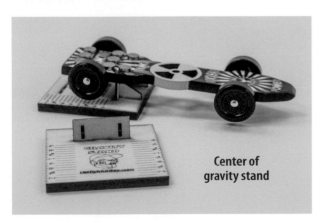

Wheel trimmer

Polishing mandrel and compound

Bore polisher tool and compound

Center of gravity stand

Axle bender

DECORATING YOUR CAR

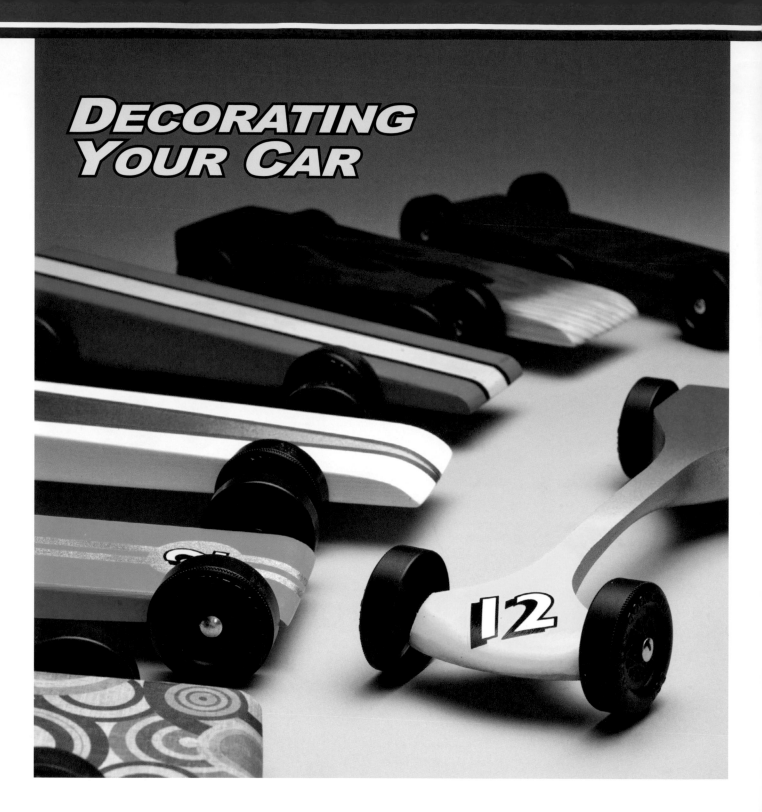

You can use almost any type of marker, paint, sticker, or tape to decorate your car. Use your imagination and see what you have around the house before you spend money on new decorations.

For a fast-drying finish that cleans up with soap and water, apply acrylic paint with a brush. Acrylic paint is thick enough that it will only take one or two coats. You can apply it with regular paintbrushes or disposable foam brushes. Foam brushes leave fewer brush strokes, but regular paintbrushes make it easier to get into tight spacers.

TIP: This technique assumes that the stripe will be lighter than the rest of the car. If you want a darker stripe, paint the light color first, and mask off both sides of the stripe before painting it.

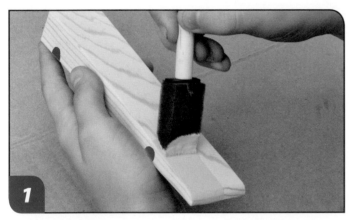

Paint the light color first. Protect the axle holes or slots with painter's tape. Using a brush and acrylic paint, paint the top of the car with the color for the center stripe. Allow the paint to dry for an hour. If desired, use a hair dryer to speed up the drying time.

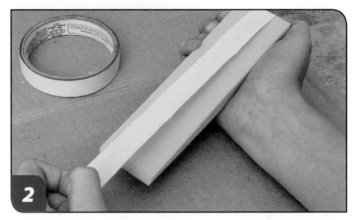

Cover the stripe. Place a piece of ¾"-wide masking tape down the center of the block. Firmly press down the tape. This will keep the second color off of the center area, creating a clean striped effect.

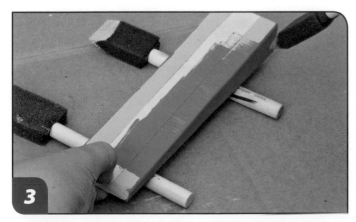

Paint the second color. Paint the second color over the entire car. Place the car over the handles of two foam brushes to raise it so you can paint down the sides. This keeps the car from sticking to the work surface. Allow the paint to dry. Then, carefully remove the masking tape from the center stripe and axle areas.

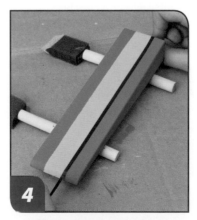

Add pinstripes. Press ⅛" pin-striping tape where the colors join to cover any areas where the paint seeped under the masking tape.

Supplies

- Acrylic paint: 2 colors
- Masking tape
- Striping tape (optional)
- Paintbrushes: 3
- Hair dryer (optional)

SPRAY PAINTING

Spray painting produces a finish similar to that of a car. The system shown is a two-step process, with a base color and a shiny clear coat. With a little practice, children can master this technique.

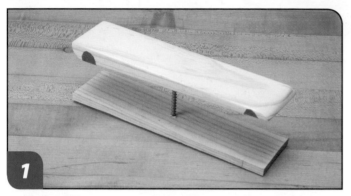

1

Prepare the car. Tape over the axle holes or slots with painter's tape. Construct a simple paint stand from a scrap of wood and a 2" screw. The stand lets you paint the entire car at the same time.

2

Apply the accent color. Place the car and stand in an open cardboard box. Begin by spraying a light coat of the accent color. This coat is the sealer and primer. Allow it to dry for 30 minutes.

3

Sand the first coat. The car will be rough after the first coat. Sand the entire surface with 220-grit sandpaper. Refold the sandpaper as it becomes covered with paint. Spray with a second coat and allow it to dry.

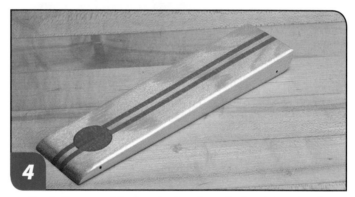

4

Apply the accent design. Apply a piece of painter's tape to a sheet of waxed paper. Trace the design, like the circle, onto the tape and cut it out. Peel the design off the waxed paper and apply it to the car. Cut two ⅛" stripes of painter's tape. Press them firmly to the car.

5

Apply the main color. Spray the main color in several light coats instead of one heavy coat. Allow the paint to dry thoroughly. Refer to the manufacturer's recommended drying time.

6

Remove the painter's tape. Remove the tape from all areas *except* the axle holes or slots. Apply several light coats of clear spray finish. Allow the car to dry completely.

AIRBRUSH PAINTING

Airbrush painting gives you the smooth finish of spray paint, but with more control. Also, you're not confined to the colors available in spray cans.

There are several affordable airbrushes on the market that are easy for children to use. In this example, we are demonstrating a simple color fading technique.

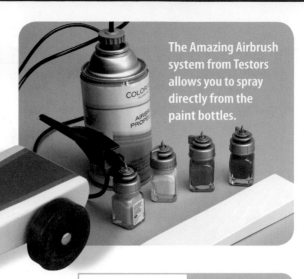

The Amazing Airbrush system from Testors allows you to spray directly from the paint bottles.

Supplies

- Masking tape
- Spray or acrylic paint (base coat)
- Airbrush kit
- Airbrush paint: 3 colors

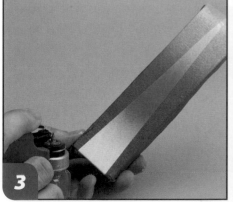

1

Mask the design. In this example, the car is already painted with a base coat of white. Use painter's tape to create a custom design. Cover the areas that you want to remain the base color. Remember to cover the axle holes or slots with painter's tape.

2

Begin to spray yellow. Begin to spray with the lightest color. Apply several thin coats only to the front of the car.

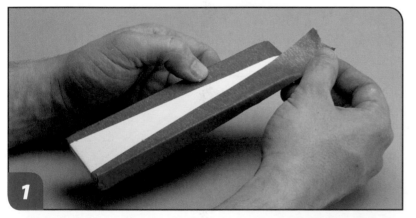

3

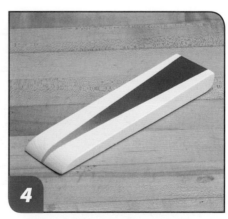

4

Build the gradient. Hold the car from the back and lightly spray the middle of the car, fading the orange into the yellow. Add the red, continuing to spray from the back of the car. Fade the red into the orange. Make sure to spray the back end of the car.

Remove the tape. Allow the car to dry thoroughly. Carefully remove the painter's tape from all areas.

PERMANENT MARKERS

Permanent markers are a quick way to make a custom finish on your car. You can choose from any of the colors in the rainbow. Make sure you don't get any marker on anything besides your car, though! It is permanent.

Supplies

• Pencil
• Permanent markers, such as Sharpie® brand

1 **Draw the design.** Use a pencil to draw your design. Start filling it in with the lightest colors.

2 **Blend the colors.** Add the next color. Before the darker color dries, rub it into the lighter color. Continue to add and blend darker colors.

3 **Outline and fill in the design.** Use a dark color to outline the light areas. Keep the marker moving so the ink won't bleed. Fill in large areas by drawing with the wood grain. This will keep all the lines going the same way and keep the finish from looking scribbled.

DUCT TAPE

Duct tape is an easy way to add color to your car without the mess of paints or markers. Many colors and patterns of tape are available at craft stores. *Note: Add weights to the car before wrapping it in duct tape (see pages 34 and 57).*

Supplies

• Duct tape
• Scissors
• Hobby knife

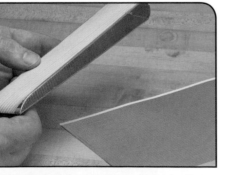

1 **Wrap the bottom of the car.** *Note: Add weights first.* Apply the tape to the bottom of the car and wrap it up the sides and back. Cut some of the tape from the corners before you wrap it to avoid thick build-up. Trim the tape even with the top of the car.

2 **Cover the top of the car.** Apply a piece of tape to the top of the car. Use scissors to trim this tape to the edges of the car.

3 **Add decorations.** Apply any decorations you would like. Use a hobby knife to remove the tape around the axle holes or slots.

STRIPING TAPE

Striping tape is a great way to add a final touch to make your car really stand out. It's also great at hiding any areas on your car that may have a flaw in the paint job, like paint that ran under a painter's tape edge.

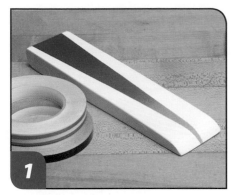

1

Select the striping tape. You can find striping tape at hobby shops or auto parts stores. Some types of striping tapes come with wide and narrow tape on the same roll.

2

Apply the tape. Cut a piece of tape longer than you need for the car. Remove the backing and align one end of the tape where you want the stripe to start. Slowly lower the tape the rest of the way onto the car.

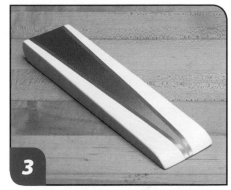

3

Press down the tape. After you apply all of the tape, go over the stripes and firmly press them onto the surface of the car.

STICKERS

Stickers are a quick and easy way to customize a car. Make a NASCAR-style car by covering it in logos or images from your favorite products, movies, or TV shows. Use sheets of letters to add a name to the car or use numbers to add your lucky number, age, or pack number.

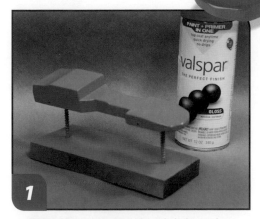

1

Paint the car. Protect the axle holes or slots with masking tape. Spray or brush the car with paint and let it dry thoroughly.

2

Apply the stickers. Plan the design by cutting around the stickers with scissors, leaving the backing in place. When you like the design, peel the backing off and attach the stickers.

Many things go into making a fast car. It's safe to say that no car is going to win races right out of the box. As with most things, the more work you put in, the faster your car will be. But there are ways to work smarter rather than harder. This section will explain the science behind fast cars, describe the basic modifications you need to make, and detail the extra steps that can make your car a winner.

THE PRINCIPLES OF SPEED

(weight) Mass

Gravity

$$\frac{Mass\ (weight)}{\times\ \frac{Gravitational\ Pull}{Height}}$$

Potential Energy

Height

Fast cars all have four things in common. Every worthwhile speed tip works to give your car the maximum benefit from each of these four principles.

1 **Design the Car with Care**

2 **Adding Weight Adds Energy**

3 **Polish and Lubricate to Reduce Friction**

4 **Align the Wheels**

Because we can't change gravity, and the height of the track is fixed, we need to maximize mass (weight) and put it in the right place to create a fast car.

1 Design the Car with Care

The car can be any shape your child chooses. However, you will need to strategically remove wood and leave extra wood to be sure the car is well balanced and that there's room for weights. You will also need to take the mechanics of the track into account (the starting peg, the timing system, etc.). See page 30 for details.

What about aerodynamics? The other principles play a greater role in the overall speed of the car. A block of wood with well-polished wheels will move faster than a specially shaped car with no wheel prep. But, having a fast-looking car gets your child in the right mind-set, and an aerodynamic shape might make a difference in a race of well-designed cars.

2 Adding Weight Adds Energy

You can think of gravity as the engine in your car—it provides the energy that makes the car roll down the track. Before the race begins, when your car is sitting at the top of the track, it has what is called potential energy. Potential energy is created through a combination of gravity, height, and mass (weight). Cars with more potential energy roll faster as they move down the track.

To maximize the amount of potential energy in your car, place the weight toward the back, use as much weight as possible (page 32), and place the weights to create a perfect balance point (page 34). A well-balanced car with the weight in the back has more potential energy because the weight has farther to travel to reach the ground.

3 Polish and Lubricate to Reduce Friction

Your car might have tons of potential energy, but not all of that energy gets converted into speed. Some energy is converted into heat as surfaces rub against each other, causing friction. The major sources of friction are the inside rims of the wheels striking the track guides, the wheel tread riding down the track, the wheel bore rotating on the axle shafts, the wheels rubbing against the axle heads, the wheel hubs rubbing against the sides of the car, and the friction of air flowing against the car as it rolls down the track.

Most speed tips, such as polishing the axles (page 37) and lubricating the wheels (pages 41–44), are aimed at reducing friction and making your car rocket down the track.

4 Align the Wheels

If the car bounces off the guide rail as it travels down the track, it will lose speed every time it touches the rail. Similarly, the friction created if the car wobbles back and forth when it hits the flat part of the track is like putting on the brakes. A finely aligned car will look like it's accelerating down the flat part of the track because it isn't losing as much speed as the unaligned cars. Read the sections about alignment (pages 45–51) to be sure the wheels on your car are perfectly adjusted and ready to race.

DESIGN THE CAR WITH CARE

There are endless choices when you are designing a Pinewood Derby car. You can build race cars or cars shaped like buses, bikes, hot dogs, or even pencils; you are only limited by your imagination. You'll be amazed by all of the creative ideas you see at the races you attend. However, to build a speedy car, it is best to stick with simpler designs that maximize the design ideas explained in this book.

Remember to include your child in the design discussions and decisions—this isn't your car, it's his or hers. Use the design process as an opportunity to teach your child about these speed and design principles. If your child has his or her heart set on a design that isn't inherently fast, use these tips to maximize the design's potential.

This aerodynamic design maximizes weight placement by removing wood from the front and center of the car.

Maximize the Dimensions

The dimensions of the car must remain within the width, height, length, and weight specifications listed in your local Derby rules. The official Boy Scouts of America (BSA®) specifications are outlined on page 12. However, you don't want to make the car shorter than the maximum length. A shorter car's weight won't be as high on the track as a longer car's will, lowering the potential energy (see page 29). Stick with car designs that use the total length of the block of wood.

Use the full length of the block to maximize potential energy.

Extend the Wheelbase

If your pack's rules allow the wheelbase to be changed from the supplied slots in the block of wood, it's best to extend the wheelbase as far as you can without the wheel treads extending past the ends of the car. A long wheelbase allows you to put the weight all the way to the back and still have a perfect center of balance, which keeps the car on the track (see page 34).

Extend the wheel base to maximize the amount of weight you can put in the back.

Choose an Aerodynamic Design

Although wheel prep and lubrication matter more than the actual design of the car, when all other things are equal, a low, sleek design usually wins. A thin, or "low profile" shape allows air to move over and around the car body in a smooth manner. This will give you two advantages: first, the car will be very aerodynamic, and second, the car body will weigh very little so you can move even more weight to the rear of the car.

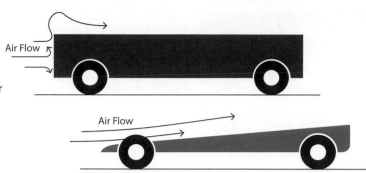

An aerodynamic design allows the air to move over and around the car body in a smooth manner. The most basic aerodynamic design is the simple wedge (bottom). If you don't have a lot of time available, the wedge is a proven design used by many Pinewood Derby winners (see the pattern on page 60).

Avoid a Round Front

Avoid any designs with a narrow, pointy nose. They will not sit against the starting pin and may be disqualified from the race. Also, any car that has a slot cut into the front to allow part of the car past the starting pin might be disqualified. Also, be sure it's clear which end is the front. Race officials usually place the cars on the track, and you don't want them to put the car on the track backwards.

Indented or pointed-nose designs, such as these, can cause problems with the pins at the starting gate and with electronic timing systems.

Leave Room for the Weights

Cars with most of their weight in the rear go faster (see page 32). Your design needs to leave enough wood at the back of the car so you can drill holes—either from the side or the bottom—to hold the weights. The type of weights you choose will determine how much room you will need. Tungsten is the densest type of weight and will require the least space to install. Lead will require over a third more space to achieve the same weight as tungsten. See page 33 for an explanation of the different types of weights and recommendations for proper placement.

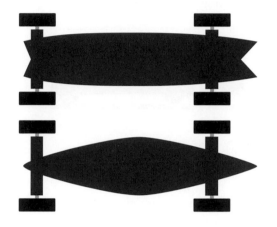

Focus the weight by drilling holes in the rear car body and filling them with weights.

Consider a Flat Bottom

If your pack's track uses a ramp braking area at the end, you may want to consider a design with a flat bottom. If your design has an arch between the wheels, your speedy car will have far less area making contact with the rubber strips on the braking ramps. The car won't slow smoothly and might flip off the end of the track, which is never a good thing for the wheel alignment!

Choose a flat bottom for your car so the braking ramps can safely stop your racer.

ADDING WEIGHT ADDS ENERGY

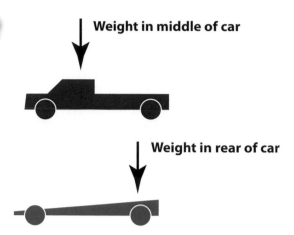

Weight in middle of car

Weight in rear of car

The two most important rules dealing with weight and weight placement are: 1) the heavier your car is, the faster it will go, and 2) rear-weighted cars go faster. By placing the weight in the rear of the car, you increase the potential energy of the car when it's at the starting gate. In other words, the "engine" propelling your car down the track stays on longer.

WHY IT WORKS

You can actually see the result of placing the weight in the rear of the car: such cars appear to accelerate at the bottom of the track where the ramp levels out. What's happening is that a front-weighted car stops accelerating when the weight reaches the flat part of the track. The weight is no longer falling, so from that point on, the car is slowing down. A rear-weighted car, on the other hand, will accelerate until the back of the car reaches the flat portion of the track because the car falls until all of its mass (weight) is on the flat portion of the track. Think of the weight as pushing the car as long as it's falling.

CHOOSING WEIGHTS

Several different types of weights are available, and all of them come in a variety of shapes.

● Recommended: Tungsten

Most Derby car experts strongly recommend using tungsten weights. A nontoxic metal, tungsten is very dense so it adds a lot of weight in a small amount of space. This makes it ideal for weighting thin cars. Although tungsten is the most expensive

option, it is the best choice for building a competitive car. If you are going to spend money on one thing, spend it on tungsten weights, which are available at some craft and hobby stores and via online retailers.

For the fastest and easiest car, use shaped tungsten weights, such as canopies and cylinders, for the main weight, and use tungsten disks or putty for the final weight adjustment.

● Use with caution: Lead

Lead is the next densest weight. It is widely available, it comes in a variety of sizes and shapes, and it is reasonably priced. However, lead is a toxic substance. Never melt or sand lead. Wear latex gloves or wash your hands thoroughly after handling lead. Keep lead out of the reach of children.

If you choose to use lead, use egg-shaped sinkers and lead wire for the main weights and split shot for the final adjustments.

● Not recommended: Zinc

Zinc weights, such as the breakable bars sold at craft stores, are inexpensive and easy to install. However, they are also about half as dense as lead so you need a lot of them to weight a car properly. It is difficult to place zinc weights effectively, especially on a thin car.

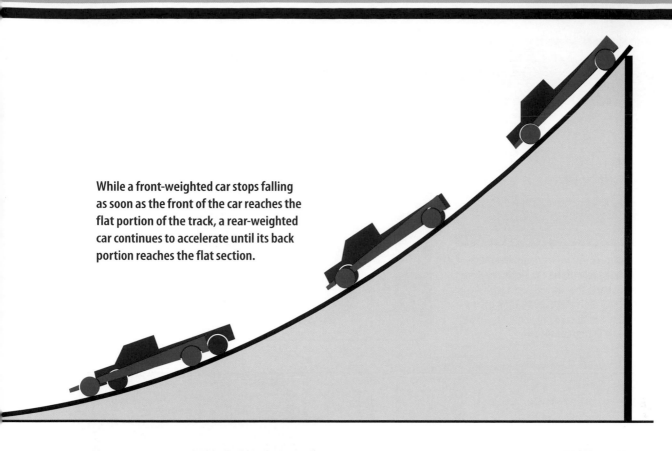

While a front-weighted car stops falling as soon as the front of the car reaches the flat portion of the track, a rear-weighted car continues to accelerate until its back portion reaches the flat section.

TUNGSTEN: RECOMMENDED

Tungsten canopies
- Easy to install
- Adds to the design
- Available in two weights
- Non-toxic

Tungsten slotted discs
- Adjust the weight by adding 2–3 tungsten cubes
- Fits into a 1" drilled hole
- Available in two weights
- Non-toxic

Tungsten putty
- Can be molded into different spaces
- Useful to fine tune center balance
- Can be used in the trim holes
- Non-toxic

Tungsten cubes
- Packs a lot of weight in a tight space
- Easy to adjust the weight
- Can be placed very low in your car
- Non-toxic

Tungsten bars
- Slim profile: excellent for thin-bodied cars
- Can be screwed onto car body
- Non-toxic

Tungsten cylinders
- Very dense
- Available in three weights
- Fits in drilled holes
- Non-toxic

LEAD: USE CAUTION

Lead Wire
- Easy to seal inside your car
- Cheaper than tungsten
- Doesn't require shaping or melting
- Toxic: use with caution

Lead split shot
- Useful to fine-tune center balance
- Available at all fishing shops
- Soft; can be pressed into holes
- Toxic: use with caution

Egg-Shaped Lead Sinkers
- Useful as main weights
- Available at all fishing shops
- Soft; can be pressed into holes
- Toxic: use with caution

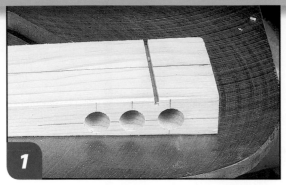

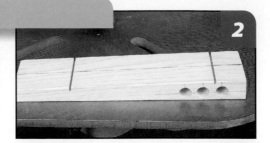

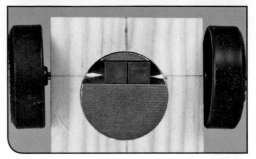

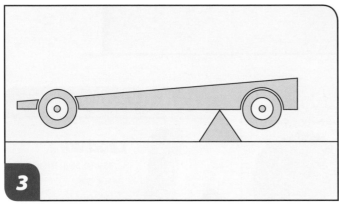

Mark the hole locations. We've seen the advantage of putting the weight in the rear of the car. However, if you put the weight too far back, the car will pop a wheelie as it goes down the track, or it might even jump off the track. Place about a third of the weight behind the rear axle and two-thirds just in front of the axle.

Drill the holes. For canopies and shaped weights, you'll generally drill a hole through the car just in front of the rear axle. Turn the car upside down and drill through the bottom into a piece of scrap wood, then sand the top again. If you're using cylinders, lead wire, or sinkers, drill holes in the sides or back and bottom of the car near the rear axle. Drill one additional hole near the front in case you need to add more weight on race day. Position slotted discs across the axle slot.

Check the center of gravity. A properly weighted car will balance on a ruler, dowel, or center of gravity stand placed about 1" in front of the rear wheel axle. Check the center of gravity often as you add weights.

Weigh the car. Place the car, axles, wheels, and weights on a digital scale. Add small weights until the scale reads 4.8 ounces, which leaves 0.2 ounces for paint, decals, and putty. If the car is slightly under weight on race day, add tungsten putty or thin disks, or lead split shot, secured with cyanoacrylate (CA) glue, such as Super Glue™.

Seal the weights into the car. Put the weights in their respective holes. You can glue a slotted disc, canopy, or decorative top weight in place. Cylinders, sinkers, and lead wire should be about 1/16" below the surface of the car. Mix a small amount of lightweight, fast-drying wood filler or putty. Use the filler or putty carefully—if the car is too heavy at the official weigh-in, you'll have to find a way to remove some weight. Apply the putty to the car, allowing it to fill the weight holes. Then, set the car aside and allow the filler to dry according to the manufacturer's instructions. Then, sand the filler flush with the car. Start with a file and then use 220- or 400-grit sandpaper. Wipe off any dust with a soft cloth.

POLISH AND LUBRICATE TO REDUCE FRICTION

Every time the wheels touch the track or the body of the car, friction causes them to slow down just a bit. Therefore, to have a competitive car, you need to remove as much friction as possible. That means smoothing, polishing, and lubricating the axles and wheels.

This is a great time for your child to do a major portion of the work—just make sure he understands why he is performing each step in the building process.

NOTE: Follow the numbered tips in this section step by step, in order. Most of them can be accomplished with household items. The Speed Secrets are optional bonus adjustments or alternate procedures that may require the purchase of additional tools or materials. Speed Secrets are inserted into the instructions at the appropriate time; for example, you should straighten the axles (below) before doing Step 1 (page 36).

TIP

CHECK YOUR LOCAL RULES

If one of the speed tips is not allowed in your Derby, don't use it. If you want to use a particular speed tip but you aren't sure whether it's legal, clear it with your local race organizer. Be honest—it's the Scouting way!

SPEED SECRET

Straighten the axle.

Insert the axle in one half of the press with the tapered head against the dimple. Use the guide rods to position the other half on top of the axle. Double check the alignment of the press and then tap it firmly a few times with a hammer. Rotate the axle slightly and tap again. Repeat the process several times to create perfectly straight axles.

Supplies
- Axle press
- Hammer

Pro Axle Press

REMOVE THE BURRS

Every official BSA axle comes out of the box with small burrs under its head. Whenever the wheel and the axle head touch, the burrs create friction and act like brakes, so you must remove them.

Supplies

- Cordless drill, drill press, or rotary tool: Used only to hold the axle. Place a drill/ rotary tool upright and weight with a sandbag to stabilize, or clamp in a vise.
- Triangular file or homemade sanding sticks (see page 18)

A

Secure an axle in a drill. Leave about ½" exposed. For this process we will only be using the drill to hold the axle. You will not be spinning the axle.

B

File away the burrs. Do not turn on the drill. Use a homemade sanding stick or a triangular file to remove the burrs. Apply only light pressure on the file so you do not bend or damage the axle while removing the burrs.

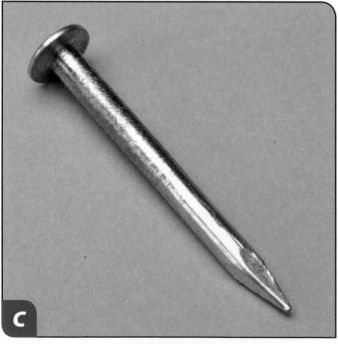

C

Remove the burrs under the head of the axle. File off any burrs on the tip of the axle also, so as not to enlarge the holes or slots in the block. The finished axles should look like this.

SPEED TIP

DON'T POLISH WITH PUMICE

Some guides call for using a paste made of pumice, but this is a bad idea. Pumice is the equivelent of 1800-grit sandpaper. Not only is it messy, but it is too fine to tackle the scratches left behind by 600-grit sandpaper. Avoid pumice and use successively finer grits of sandpaper instead.

2 POLISH THE AXLES

Wheels rubbing on the axles creates the largest source of friction on the car. The fastest way to make a fast car is to reduce this friction and make the axle as smooth as possible.

When you've finished sanding, your axles should look like this.

Supplies

- Cordless drill, drill press, or rotary tool: Stabilize with sandbags or clamp in a vise as needed.
- Wet/dry sandpaper: 400, 600, & 1000 grit (Optional: 1200, 1500, 2000, 2500, & 3000-grit paper and 2 and 1 micron aluminum oxide polishing paper, available in most auto parts stores.)
- Magnifying glass
- Scissors
- Water

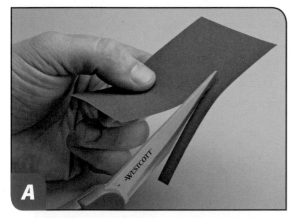

A

Make polishing strips. Cut a strip about ¼" wide and 4" long from each of the sandpaper grits. Write the grit numbers on the backs of the strips.

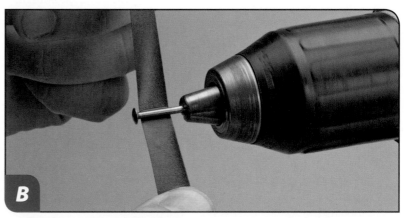

B

Sand the axle. Dip a strip of 400-grit sandpaper in a small dish of water. Turn the drill on medium to high speed and then apply the sandpaper to the axle. Sand the entire axle, including the inside surface of the head. This step should take about 15 seconds. Turn off the drill. *Warning: Excessive polishing will reduce the diameter of the axle shaft.*

C

Check your progress. Look at the axle with a good magnifying glass. Check for deep scratches. Turn the drill back on and polish again. Repeat the process until all of the deep scratches have been removed.

D

Repeat Steps B and C. Use 600 and then 1000-grit sandpaper. Look at the axle with a magnifying glass after each step to be sure the axle shaft is as smooth as it can be. If you like, repeat the steps using 1200-, 1500-, 2000-, 2500-, and 3000-grit sandpaper and then 2 and 1 micron polishing paper. (Do not use water with the micron paper.)

Taper the Axle Head

As the axle head and the wheel rub against each other, they create friction and slow the car down. Tapering the head of the axle makes the area of the axle head that touches the wheel much smaller.

Supplies

- Cordless drill, drill press, or rotary tool: Stabilize with sandbags or clamp in a vise.
- Flat smooth-tooth file
- Wet/dry sandpaper: 400 grit
- Scissors
- Water

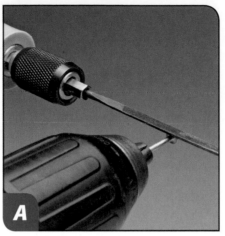

Gently file a 5° angle onto the axle head. Use a smooth-tooth file. Do not turn the drill on.

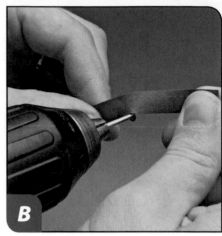

Remove the file scratches. Cut a ¼" wide by 4" long strip of 400-grit sandpaper. Dip the strip into water, and then use it to polish the tapered axle head. Do not turn the drill on.

Make Grooved Axles

Reducing the contact between the wheel and the axle improves the performance of your car. If you cut a groove in the axle, the grooved area will never touch the wheel. Plus, the groove becomes a secret trough where lubricant gets stored. During the race, some of the lubricant will work its way out of the trough and lubricate the inside of the wheel. *Not every pack allows grooved axles, so check your pack's rules.* Some Derby suppliers sell pre-grooved axles.

Supplies

- Drill press
- Ruler
- Marker
- Flat file

Mark the axles. Place a mark on the axle ¹⁄₁₆" from the axle head. Place a second mark ³⁄₁₆" from the head.

Clamp the axle in a drill press chuck. Line up the drill press table with the marks you made on the axle. Use a file to make sure everything is aligned.

Use a flat file to cut the groove. Set the drill press to a low speed. Use the flat file to gently cut a ¹⁄₆₄"-deep groove. Don't cut the groove too deep; it will weaken the axle.

Polish the axle. Use the techniques explained on the previous pages until the axle is smooth and polished.

PREPARING THE WHEEL HUBS

A

Reem the axle holes. Not every axle hole is fully formed. Use the Pro Hub Tool to remove any large imperfections from the inside of the hub.

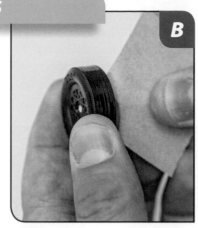

B

Square up the inner hub. Press the end of the Pro Hub Tool with the square shoulder down against a piece of 220-grit sandpaper to cut a precise center hole. Slide the sandpaper down to the square shoulder and remove some of the excess sandpaper. Insert the hub tool into the axle hole with the inner hub against the square shoulder. Rotate the wheel a few times to square up the edges of the hub with the axle hole. Repeat the process with increasingly finer grits of sandpaper to smooth and polish the hub.

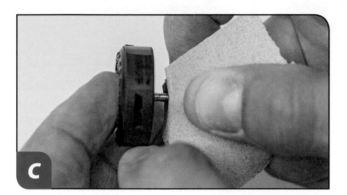

C

Sand the inner hub to a cone shape. This reduces friction. Check to make sure your pack allows coned hubs. Secure 220-grit sandpaper in the tapered end of the Pro Hub Tool. Insert the hub tool into the axle hole and press the inner hub of the wheel firmly against the tapered shoulder as you rotate to give the inner hub a cone shape. Repeat the process with increasingly finer grits of sandpaper to smooth and polish the hub.

Supplies

- Pro Hub Tool
- Pro Hub Shaver
- Pro Wheel Shaver
- Sandpaper: 220–400 grits

TRUING THE WHEELS

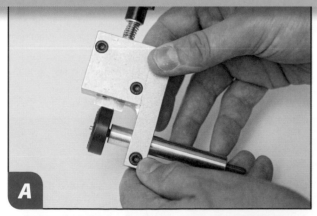

A

Determine which wheel is most out of round (true). Secure the Pro Hub Tool in the Pro Hub Shaver with ½" of the shoulder exposed. Place a wheel on the Pro Hub Tool and move the cutter down until it just touches the wheel as the wheel revolves. Remove the wheel, and repeat the process with the other wheels. This determines which wheel is most out of round. We will start the shaving process with this wheel.

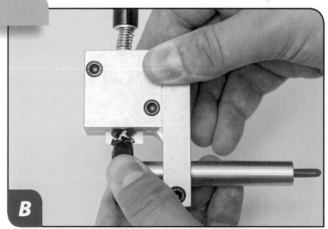

B

Shave the wheels down to perfectly round (true). Set the cutter to remove a very small amount. Rotate the wheel a few times to remove the high spot. Then, move on to the next wheel. Repeat the process with the other wheels before returning to the first one. Move the cutter in a very small amount and rotate the wheel again. Repeat the process with the other wheels. Then, repeat the entire process until the cutter is removing a small amount from the entire surface of all of the wheels, ensuring all four are perfectly round.

3 SMOOTH THE WHEELS

Remove the defects on stock wheels by sanding them using a wheel mandrel. This handy tool is available at most BSA Scout Shops, www.scoutstuff.org, and a many online retailers (see Resources on page 94). Do not attempt to sand the wheels without using a wheel mandrel. You will only create problems for your car.

Mount the wheel. Attach a wheel to a mandrel. Place the mandrel in an electric drill or a Dremel tool. Then, attach a piece of 600-grit wet/dry sandpaper to a flat block of wood. Moisten the sandpaper.

Smooth the wheel. Turn on the drill or rotary tool and allow the spinning wheel to rub gently against the sandpaper. Add more water to the paper when it starts to look dry. The plastic will become hot and melt unless you keep the sandpaper damp and maintain minimal pressure. (Too much pressure can deform the wheels.) Sand until the mold bubble is gone and the wheel looks smooth.

4 SMOOTH THE RIMS

As your car rolls down the track, the inside wheel rim will occasionally make contact with the center guide rail, so you need to make the inside rim as smooth as it can be. Polishing the rim will reduce friction.

Mount the wheel. Attach the wheel to a wheel mandrel and then spin the wheel using a power drill or a Dremel tool.

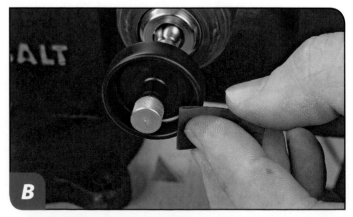

Smooth the rim. Gently sand the inside wheel rim using 400-, 600-, and then 1000-grit sandpaper.

POLISH THE WHEEL BORES

Polishing the wheel bore will reduce the friction between the wheel and the axle as the car rolls down the track.

A

Mount a pipe cleaner. Cut a 5" section of pipe cleaner and place it through one of the wheels. Insert and secure the pipe cleaner in the drill or rotary tool.

B

Apply toothpaste. Push the wheel toward the drill and coat the pipe cleaner with whitening toothpaste. Whitening toothpaste contains a fine abrasive polish.

C

Smooth the bore. Hold the wheel between your fingers and turn on the drill using medium speed. Slowly move the wheel up and down the pipe cleaner as it spins. Polish each wheel for about 45 seconds (don't over-polish).

D

Wash the bore. Turn off the drill and remove the wheel from the pipe cleaner. Using warm water and a clean pipe cleaner, wash the wheel thoroughly. Remove all of the toothpaste from inside the wheel bore.

E

Dry the bore. Using another clean dry pipe cleaner, dry the inside of the bore. Do not leave any water droplets inside the bore. If water droplets remain, they may leave residue behind as they dry.

Advanced Wheel Bore Polishing

This procedure replaces Step 5.

This advanced polishing technique goes beyond basic wheel bore preparation. It will put a super-smooth surface on the inside of the wheel bore and significantly reduce the surface contact friction. You'll only need a few tools and supplies, most of which you may already have lying around the house. If not, you can find them in most stores or through a Pinewood Derby specialty store.

— Steve Robbins of Derby Monkey

Supplies

- Cordless drill, drill press, or rotary tool: Stabilize with sandbags or clamp in a vise as needed.
- Pipe cleaners
- Cotton swabs with paper handle, such as a Q-Tip brand
- Liquid polish: Brasso, Turtle Wax, Derby Worx Micro-Polish, or Micro-Gloss abrasive
- Fine liquid polish: Micro-Surface Finishing Products' Micro-Finish Polish
- Wax: Meguiar's Tech wax, Liquid Glass Auto Polish, or Derby Worx Pro Bore Wax
- Derby Worx Pro Bore Polisher (optional)

See Resources, pg. 94.

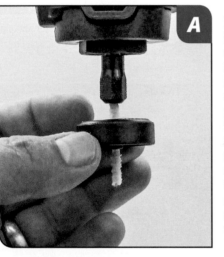

A

Polish the inside of the bore. Use a liquid polish such as Brasso, Turtlewax Liquid Polish, Derby Worx Micro-Polish, or Micro-Gloss abrasive. Test the polish on a spare wheel to make sure it doesn't react to the plastic. Chuck a 2"-long piece of pipe cleaner in the drill, apply the polish to the pipe cleaner, turn on the drill at a low speed, and polish the inner wheel bore for 10 seconds.

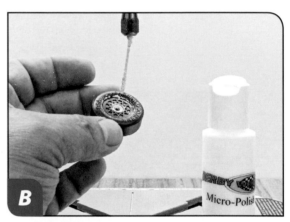

B

Refine the inside of the bore. Repeat Step 1 using a fresh pipe cleaner and finer liquid polish, such as Micro-Surface Finishing Products' Micro-Finish Polish.

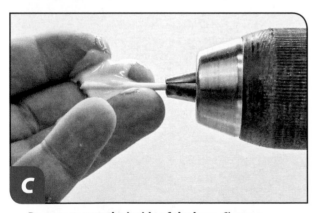

C

Prepare to wax the inside of the bore. Choose a cotton swab with a paper stick. Cut the cotton tips off both ends, cutting one off at an angle. The paper shaft fits tightly into the wheel bores. Chuck the stick in a hand-held variable-speed drill. Apply a high-quality liquid wax, such as Meguiar's Tech Wax, Liquid Glass Auto Polish, or Derby Worx Pro Bore Wax, to the inside of the bore and the outside of the paper stick.

D

Wax the inside of the bore. Turn on the drill at its lowest setting and insert the stick into the wheel bore. Increase the drill to medium speed and polish the wheel bore for 15 seconds. Allow the wheel to dry for at least two hours. Carefully remove any waxy residue from the bore with a pipe cleaner. Insert the pipe cleaner slightly into the bore and rotate around the circumference of the bore. Do not move the pipe cleaner back and forth. If you inspect the wheel bore under lighted magnification, you should see a highly polished surface.

6 LUBRICATE THE WHEELS

The same way car engines and other machines use oil to reduce friction, we need to apply lubricant to your Derby car to reduce friction. Liquid lubricants are not allowed, so we use powdered graphite instead.

Supplies

- Pipe cleaners: Soft cotton (available at tobacco and some craft stores)
- Rag: soft cloth
- Graphite lubricant (available at Scout and craft stores)

A

Grab a clean, soft cloth. Place a small amount of graphite on the corner.

B

Roll the inside rim of the wheel on the graphite pile. Apply light pressure to buff the graphite onto the edge. Continue buffing the edge until it's shiny and smooth. Repeat for the remaining three wheels.

C

Rub graphite onto the hub. Apply light pressure to buff the graphite until the hub is smooth and shiny. Repeat for the remaining three wheels.

D

Cover a soft pipe cleaner with graphite. Insert the pipe cleaner into the wheel bore and buff the wheel bore until it's shiny. Repeat all steps for the remaining three wheels.

SPEED TIP

DON'T LUBRICATE WITH WHITE TEFLON® POWDER

White Teflon powder was introduced some years ago as an alternative to graphite. Teflon works in frying pans, so it should work on Pinewood Derby wheels, right? Absolutely not. Teflon powder doesn't lubricate wheels as well as graphite.

STOP

Paint or Decorate Your Car Before You Continue.

See pages 22–27 for ideas and instructions.

See pages 22–27 for ideas and instructions.

TIP

MASK THE WHEEL WELLS BEFORE PAINTING THE CAR

Before you paint, cut pieces of painter's tape to cover the axle holes. You don't want paint or anything else clogging the holes and adding friction.

7   LUBRICATE THE WHEEL WELLS

In this step we will be applying graphite to the area around the axle hole. You should paint or finish your car as desired before doing these steps.

Supplies

- Painted car
- Blue painter's tape
- Sandpaper: 600 grit
- Graphite lubricant
- Rag: soft cloth
- WD-40 (optional)
- Magnifying glass

A **Remove the painter's tape.** Lightly sand all four wheel well areas with 600-grit sandpaper.

B **Cover the painted area around the wheel well with painter's tape.** This will keep the paint clean. Apply the graphite to a smooth piece of cloth and gently rub it into the wood around the axle hole. Continue to apply graphite until the area looks as smooth as it can be. Lubricate all four wheel wells.

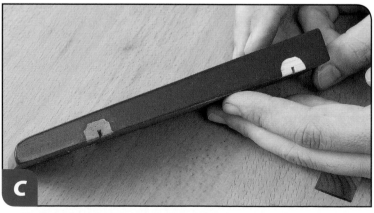

C **Check your work.** Use a magnifying glass to be sure you don't have any big scratches or bumps. If you do, sand them down and reapply the graphite. Once you are happy with the area, remove the tape.

TIP

REMOVING GRAPHITE

If you get some graphite on the paint, use a little WD-40® on a rag to wipe it off. Don't spray WD-40 on the paint because you could ruin the finish.

ATTACH & ALIGN THE WHEELS

Properly aligning the wheels is critical to creating a competitive car. First, we will bend the axles so we can control the wheel alignment and adjust the rear wheels. Then, we'll discuss two methods for aligning the front wheels: the straight alignment method and the Rail Riding™ method. Both methods have advantages and difficulties. Read the instructions and then choose one method to align your car's front wheels for top performance.

NOTE: Follow the numbered tips in this section step by step, in order. Most of them can be accomplished with household items. The Speed Secrets are optional bonus adjustments or alternate procedures that may require the purchase of additional tools or materials

1 PREPARE A TEST SURFACE

You might think that making a test track is a waste of time, but it is actually crucial to your success. You have to see how the car performs in order to fine tune it and create a winning racer. You can use a table, shelving, PVC, or a purchased test track. Elevate one end so the car will roll and put a soft pillow or blanket at the other end to stop the car gently.

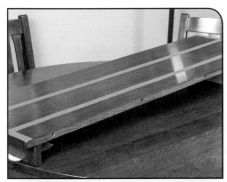

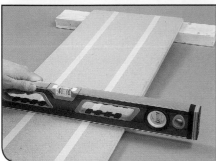

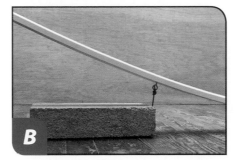

Method 1: Create a simple test track. Start with table leaves (or the whole table), lengths of shelving, or strips of plywood/MDF. Tape parallel lines 5" to 6" apart. Slightly raise one end and put a towel or pillow at the other end. Be sure the test track is level across its width.

Method 2: Create a small-scale race track. You'll need 2 pieces of ¼" x 1½" x 8' PVC lattice strip, 2 pieces of ¾" x 3½" x 8' PVC trim plank, 8–10 ½"-long lath screws, 1 #8 x 1⅝" screw eye, 3' of lightweight rope, several wooden shims, and some tape. (A) Screw each piece of PVC lattice strip to the center of a PVC trim plank. Space the screws 24" apart. (B) Attach the screw eye to the bottom of the track about 3' from one end. Tie the rope to the screw eye. Prop one end of the track about 2' off the ground. Pull the rope down toward the ground and place a heavy object on top of it to give the track a smooth bend. (C) Tape the two lengths of track end to end and place the shims underneath to support it. Put a towel or pillow at the end to catch the car.

Method 1:

The first step in any alignment, either straight or Rail Riding, is bending, or "canting," the axles. Canting the axles has a few advantages as compared to using flat, or straight, axles. First, only part of the wheel's tread surface will be touching the track, so there's less wheel friction. Second, the canting will cause the wheel to rise against the axle head and not bounce back and forth between the axle head and the car body. Last, but not least, the bends in the axles will allow you to make adjustments to the wheels that will allow you to control how the car rolls down the track. The rear wheels should be canted at an angle of 2.5° and the front wheels should be canted at an angle of 1.5°.

Supplies

- Polished wheels
- Axles
- Marker
- Vise
- Flathead screwdriver
- Hammer

An alternative to bending axles is to drill angled axle holes. While you can drill the angled holes with a drill press, Pinewood Pro's Pro Axle Driller allows you to drill holes at a 2.5° angle using a hand drill.

NOTE

Some packs are now disallowing canted wheels; they require that wheel treads stay flat on the track. A bend of 2.5° will usually lift the outside of the tread. Therefore, if pack rules require full tread contact with the track, bend all of the axles 1.5° instead of 2.5°. **If bending is forbidden, skip to Step 5 and align the car as shown.**

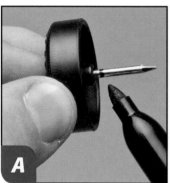

A **Mark the axle.** Insert an axle into a wheel and use a permanent marker to make a mark all around the axle shaft about 1⁄16" (1mm) behind the wheel hub. Then place a mark from the center of the axle head to the edge.

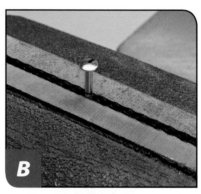

B **Place the axle into a bench vise.** Align the axle so the line on the shaft is just above the top of the vise and the line on the head points away from you.

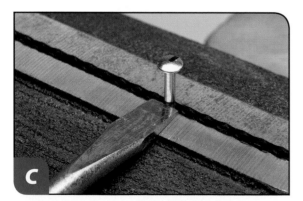

C **Bend the axle.** Place a flathead screwdriver at the base of the axle and rest it on the bench vise. Very lightly tap the end of the screwdriver with a hammer.

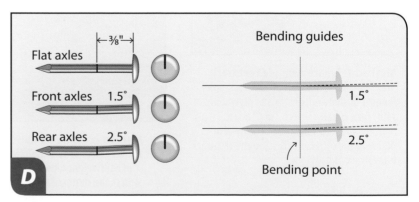

Flat axles — 3⁄8"
Front axles — 1.5°
Rear axles — 2.5°

Bending guides
1.5°
2.5°
Bending point

D **Check the axle.** Compare the axle to the drawing above to be sure it is bent 2.5°. (See note above and bend axles 1.5° if necessary.) Repeat the steps for the remaining axles.

SPEED SECRET

METHOD 2

Supplies

- Polished wheels
- Axles
- Marker
- Pro Axle Press
- Pro Rail Rider
- Hammer

See Resources, pg. 94.

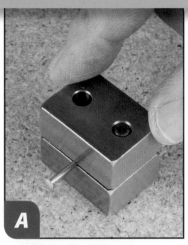

A

B

Position the axle in the press. Make an alignment dot on the head of the axle. Insert the axle in the Pro Axle Press with the alignment dot in the 6 o'clock position and the head sticking out about ½".

Bend the axle. Choose the desired angle (1.5° or 2.5°) and position the Pro Rail Rider over the axle press with that end over the exposed axle. Carefully align the slot in the Pro Rail Rider with the shaft of the axle. Make sure the alignment dot is still at the 6 o'clock position. Hold the axle head firmly against the tool and tap the top of the Pro Rail Rider a few times to bend the axle.

METHOD 3

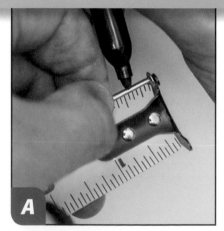

A

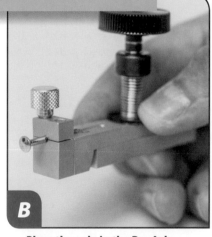

B

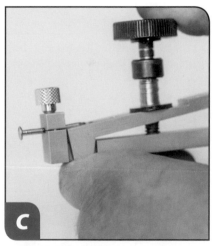

C

Mark the axle. Make an alignment dot on the axle head. Measure ⅜" down the shaft from the axle head and make a dot on the shaft. This is where the axle will be bent.

Supplies

- Polished wheels
- Axles
- Marker
- Ruler
- Pro Axle Bender
- Graphite lubricant

See Resources, pg. 94.

Place the axle in the Pro Axle Bender. Loosen the thumb screw and lift the clamp cap. Insert the axle and position the head in the appropriate indent in the lever. Position the alignment dot in the 12 o'clock position and align the dot on the shaft with the edge of the clamp cap. Tighten the thumbscrew to secure the axle. Use the hex key to loose the set screw in the spring collar and set it to the desired bending angle. Secure the set screw.

Bend the axle. Place your thumb on the black knob. Pull the lever smoothly and steadily with your index finger until the spring fully compresses and the axle is bent. Apply a little racing lubricant to the axle groove on the lever for a smoother bend.

MAKE A WHEEL SPACER

Supplies

- Empty car kit box
- Scissors
- Tape
  OR
- Purchased spacer

If you leave too much space between the wheel and car body, the wheels will shake and wobble as they turn. If you put the wheels too close to the body, the wheel hub will rub against the car almost the entire way down the track. So, we need to get the spacing right. The correct amount of space to leave between the wheel and the car body is 1/32". You can either make or buy a spacer.

Several Derby suppliers have created special tools to adjust the spacing. Most are inexpensive and more durable than a cardboard spacer, if you plan to make several cars. See the Resources on page 94.

A

Cut the cardboard. You'll need two 2" by 3" pieces of cardboard cut from the empty car kit box.

B

Tape the pieces of cardboard together. Use painter's tape along the sides. Using scissors, cut off the end of the spacer to create an even edge. Cut a 1/8"-wide by 1/4"-deep slot into this edge.

ATTACH THE WHEELS

A

Install the wheels. Place a prepared axle into a wheel. Firmly press the axle into the axle slot or axle hole. *Do not use a hammer.* The indented back end of a Sharpie® marker makes a good tool for pushing the axle into place. Use the spacer to set the gap between the wheel in the car body.

B

Check the initial alignment. Place the car on a flat surface, such as a kitchen table or a countertop. Get on your knees and look directly underneath the car. Each wheel should be resting flat and square on the table. If the wheels are not flat and square, adjust them until all four are properly positioned.

ALIGN THE REAR WHEELS

The goal for the rear wheels is to reduce friction. We don't want them to float back and forth, hitting the axle head and the body, because that creates friction and slows the car down. Instead, we'll encourage the wheels to move toward the axle head and stay there as the car rolls down the track.

TIP

DON'T OVER-ADJUST

Make the smallest adjustment necessary to get the wheels to track correctly. If you're too aggressive with the axle rotation, you will cause unnecessary toe-in or -out and that can cause a loss of speed.

Test the wheels. Point the mark on the axle head to 12 o'clock. Roll the car back and forth on your test surface.

Align the left rear wheel. Work on one wheel at a time. Move the car forward and watch the gap between the car body and the wheel hub of the left rear wheel. Refer to the diagram and use pliers to slightly rotate the axle head. Repeat the test until the wheel rolls to the axle head and stays there.

Align the right rear wheel. Repeat the process on the right wheel. Once the right wheel is rolling correctly, test them both at the same time. They should both move toward the axle head at the same time.

If the left wheel slides toward the car...

...rotate the axle clockwise.

If the right wheel slides toward the car...

...rotate the axle counter-clockwise.

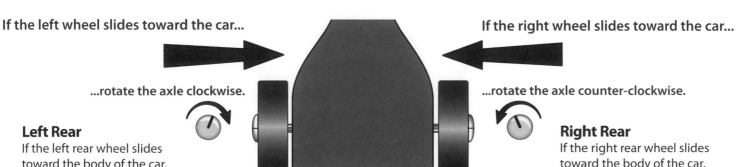

Left Rear

If the left rear wheel slides toward the body of the car, rotate the axle clockwise a few degrees. Retest the car on the test surface and continue to adjust the angle until the wheel rests against the axle head rolling the car forward and backward.

Rear wheels canted 2.5°

Right Rear

If the right rear wheel slides toward the body of the car, rotate the axle counter-clockwise a few degrees. Retest the car on the test surface and continue to adjust the angle until the wheel rests against the axle head rolling the car forward and backward.

Minimal contact with track

Rear view

Method 1: Straight Runner

There are two options for the front wheel alignment. You can set up the car to go straight down the track, known as a "straight runner," or align it so it steers into the center guide, known as a "Rail Rider." Setting your car to go straight down the track is the best option when your track doesn't have a center guide or if the center guide has rough edges. The goal is for the car to roll down the track while striking the center guide as few times as possible. Every time your car strikes the center rail, it loses speed.

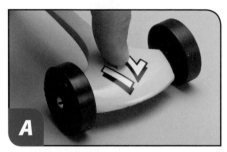

A

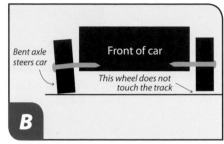

B

C

Find the wheel that steers. Place the car on a flat surface. Gently push on the front center. The car will shift toward one of the wheels. *The other wheel* carries the weight of the front of the car and is known as the steering wheel/axle. Remember which wheel is the steering wheel. It's important for the next step.

Adjust the nonsteering wheel (optional). *If your pack's rules allow it, adjust the non-steering front wheel until it does not touch the track. Skip this step if your pack's rules require all four wheels to touch the track.*

Test and adjust the steering wheel. Gently roll the car down the test track. Watch it from the back. Unless you're very lucky, the car will pull to one side or the other. Refer to the diagram below and make very small adjustments to the steering axle until your car travels straight down the center of the track.

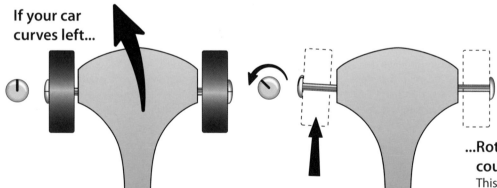

If your car curves left...

...Rotate the steering axle counter-clockwise.
This will tilt the axle bend forward, causing the car to steer right.

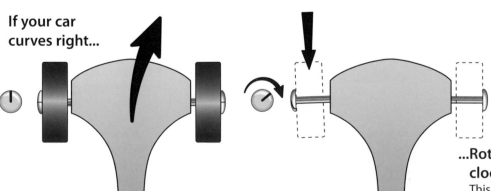

If your car curves right...

...Rotate the steering axle clockwise.
This will tilt the axle bend backward, causing the car to steer left.

NOTE

It does not matter if your left or right wheel is the steering wheel; you still rotate the axles the same direction.

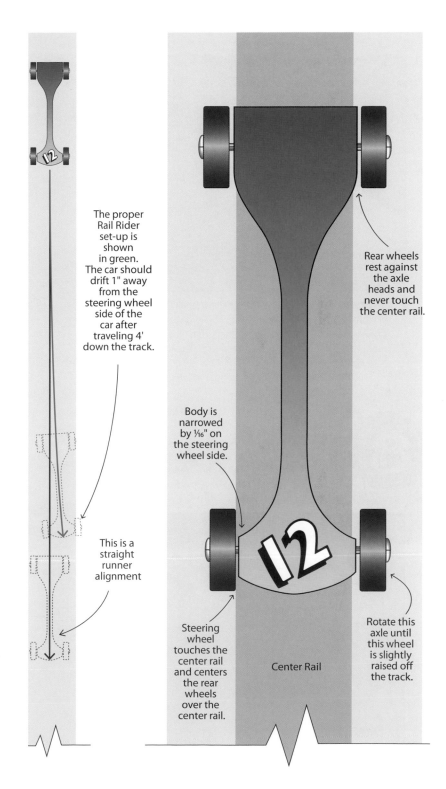

Method 2: The Rail Rider™

The second option for front wheel alignment is a technique called "Rail Riding." Credit goes to Jay Wiles for popularizing the technique and coining the term.

The idea is to steer the car into the center rail within the first few feet of the race and keep it there. The car should hug the center rail the entire way down the track, avoiding the back and forth motion that robs it of speed. There will be friction from the front wheel touching the center rail, but it will be minimal because we have already polished the inside rim of the wheel.

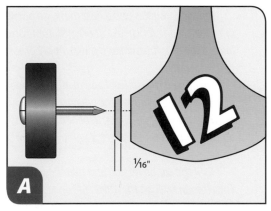

A

1/16"

Trim the car. Trim 1/16" of wood from the body on the streering wheel side of the car. This will center the rear wheels over the center rail.

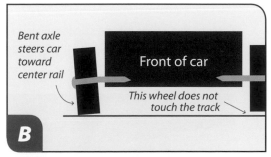

B

Bent axle steers car toward center rail

Front of car

This wheel does not touch the track

Adjust the steering wheel. Rotate the steering axle until the mark points down. This forces the wheel away from the car and encourages the car to turn in against the center rail. While this "Rail Riding" action does generate friction, the car doesn't lose as much energy as it would if the wheels were rubbing against the car body and swerving back and forth down the track.

The proper Rail Rider set-up is shown in green. The car should drift 1" away from the steering wheel side of the car after traveling 4' down the track.

This is a straight runner alignment

Rear wheels rest against the axle heads and never touch the center rail.

Body is narrowed by 1/16" on the steering wheel side.

Steering wheel touches the center rail and centers the rear wheels over the center rail.

Center Rail

Rotate this axle until this wheel is slightly raised off the track.

SPEED SECRET

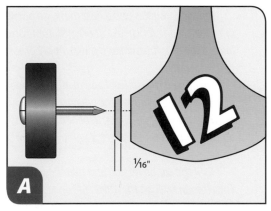
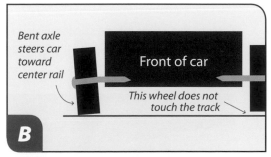

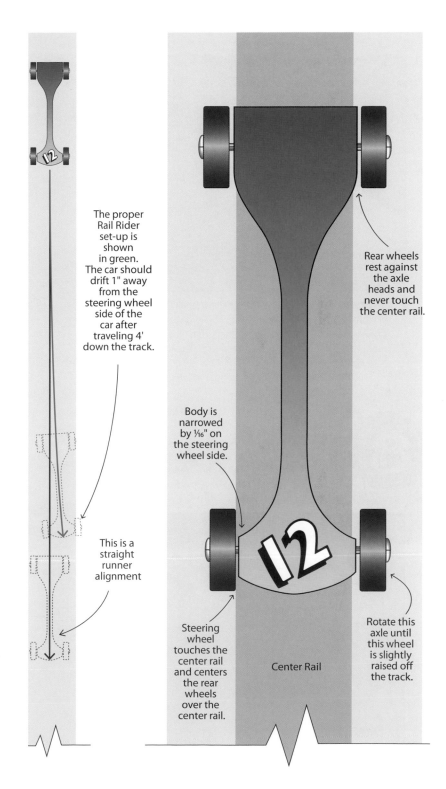

7 SET THE ALIGNMENT

Supplies

- White glue (Do not use Super Glue® or Krazy Glue®)

After the alignment is all set. Place a small dab of white glue on each axle and allow the glue to dry overnight. Do not use Super Glue®. Thin glue could travel down the axle shaft and ruin all your hard work.

8 LUBRICATE THE WHEEL BORES

Supplies

- Completed car
- Graphite lubricant
- Paintbrush: An inexpensive watercolor brush works well.
- Small bowl

Squeeze some graphite from the tube into a small dish. Dip the brush into the graphite and then gently transfer the graphite from the brush to the axle on the outside of each wheel. As you apply the graphite, gently shake or tap each wheel. This will help move the graphite down inside the wheel bore. Repeat the process on all four wheels.

SPEED TIP

PRERACE YOUR CAR

If you have ever been to a Pinewood Derby, you may have noticed that a lot of cars will not do very well their first or second time down the track. However, by the end of the Derby, those same cars will be running better and will sometimes even beat cars they lost to in the first or second heat. This isn't just your imagination playing tricks on you. As a general rule, your car will get a little faster each time it goes down the track because the wheels and axles wear into each other and get smoother. Your car will be faster the twentieth time it races than it was the first time.

So, race your car 50 or 100 times before the Pinewood Derby! How do you accomplish this without a track? It's simple—use your finger!

Wearing goggles and a dust mask, go outside or to the garage (or choose another suitable area in case the graphite makes a mess). Apply graphite to each wheel.

Then, hold the car level and gently spin one of the wheels. As you see the wheel start to slow down slightly, spin it again. Repeat this process for about 15 minutes per wheel. You may want to put in a movie.

Turn the car on its side and spin the wheels. Turn the car over on the other side and spin them. Periodically apply more graphite (after every five or 10 minutes) and continue spinning the wheels until the movie is over. When you are finished, your car will have run at least 100 races. It will be a finely tuned racing machine!

Caution: Handle the car and spin the wheels very gently so you don't ruin the alignment or dislodge the wheels or axles.

Prerace your car to break in the wheels, axles, and graphite—simply spin the wheels with your finger.

N ow that you have gathered the tools, understand the physics, and know the Speed Secrets, it's time to put it all together and build the car. This chapter will guide you through the basic steps for building a car, as well as offer 21 patterns for beginning to advanced woodworkers. Two additional step-by-step projects will help you build stylish race cars inspired by real-world automobiles. And, of course, you can always adapt the patterns and instructions to make a custom car that's all yours.

MAKING A BASIC SPEED CAR

Although this car isn't fancy, it is a competitive racer. The project is simple enough that a child can build both the car and his confidence. Your child will be proud and excited to race a car he built, and he will learn principles of woodworking and science. Making this car car will be fun and rewarding for both of you.

Don't wait until the last minute to start building the car. If you try to rush, you and your child will get frustrated with each other. A young child's attention span is only 45 minutes to an hour. Plan to work on this project over several nights.

The toughest part of this project is cutting the block of wood. If your pack or club has a work night with power tools, it would be a good idea to get help with that step. Otherwise, the only power tool you need is a drill. Remind your child to wear safety goggles and a dust mask when cutting and sanding the car, and when working with dry graphite lubricant.

This project focuses on basic techniques. For more advanced instructions, see the chapters about adding weight (page 32), polishing the axles (page 35), lubricating the wheels (page 43), and aligning the wheels (page 45).

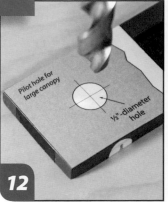

11 **Place the car, wheels, and axles on a scale.** For the best performance, the car should weigh as close to 5.0 ounces as possible. Add a large tungsten weight, such as a slotted weight or a canopy, and small weights, such as tungsten balls or thin disks, until the scale reads 4.9 ounces. That leaves a little wiggle room in case your scale doesn't match the official scale.

12 **Drill holes for the weights.** Trace the hole location from the pattern. For the canopies, you will drill through the car. For the other weights, measure the thickness and wrap a piece of masking tape around a drill bit so you know when to stop drilling. Drill an additional small hole in case you need to adjust the weight on race day.

SPEED CAR: PREP THE AXLES & WHEELS

You will need a power drill or rotary tool and an adult helper to prepare the axles and wheels.

13 **Attach the weights.** Use cyanoacrylate glue, such as SuperGlue™, to fix the weights in their holes. You can fill most of the holes if desired, but leave at least one open in case you need to add weight on race day. See page 34 for more on filling the holes.

14 **Remove the burrs from the axles.** Insert the axle into a drill or rotary tool and tighten it securely. Do not turn the drill/tool on; you are just using it to hold the axle. Use a triangular file or homemade sanding sticks to smooth the axle stem and head. See page 36 for detailed instructions. Taper the axle head if desired. See page 38 for details. Leave the last axle in the drill/tool for the next step.

TIP
MAKING SANDING STICKS

Glue sandpaper to craft sticks & trim to fit. Write the grit on the stick.

15 **Polish the axles.** Cut four strips of 400-grit wet-dry sandpaper. Dip a strip in a small bowl of water. With the drill/tool running at medium speed, sand the axle for about 15 seconds to remove the scratches and polish it. Repeat the process with 600-grit sandpaper and then as many additional grits as desired. See page 37 for detailed instructions. Add grooves to the axles if desired and your pack rules allow them (see page 38).

Secure a wheel in a wheel mandrel. Do not overtighten the wheel on the mandrel. Insert the mandrel into a cordless drill or rotary tool and tighten it securely. Tape a piece of 400-grit sandpaper to a block of wood. (Use the flat side of the scrap from the original block.)

Remove the mold marks. Wet the sandpaper. Run the drill/tool at a low speed. Apply only light pressure and sand until the wheel surface is flat and smooth. Repeat for the remaining three wheels. Leave the last axle on the mandrel in the drill/tool for the next step.

Smooth the inside rims. Run the drill/tool at a low speed. Gently sand the inside wheel rim using 400-, 600- and 1000-grit sandpaper. Repeat for the remaining three wheels.

Polish the wheel bores. Use a drill or rotary tool, a piece of good-quality pipe cleaner, and whitening toothpaste. See page 41 for detailed instructions and page 42 for an advanced polishing technique.

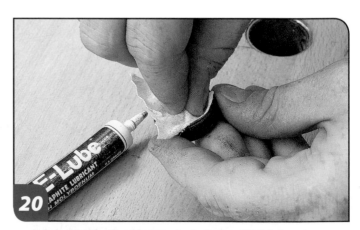

Lubricate the wheel bores. Apply dry graphite lubricant to a soft cloth and rub it into the inside rim and wheel hub. Use a good-quality pipe cleaner to apply the lubricant to the wheel bore. See page 43 for detailed instructions.

21

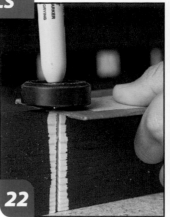

22

Lubricate the wheel wells. Mask the area around the wheel well with tape. Squeeze a small amount of dry graphite lubricant onto a paper towel. Rub the graphite over the wheel slots where the axles attach. This helps reduce friction where the wheels rub against the car. See page 44 for detailed instructions.

Attach the first wheel. Make or buy a wheel spacer. Place it between the wheel and the car. Firmly press the axle into the axle slot. The bottom end of a Sharpie marker makes a good tool to push the axle into the slot. Remove the wheel spacer and repeat for the remaining wheels. All of the wheels should be spaced an even distance from the car.

23

24

Align the wheels. After you attach all four wheels, place the car on a flat surface. Look underneath the car. If any of the wheels do not rest flat and square on the surface, adjust them until they do. If desired, refer to pages 46–51 and align the wheels

Lubricate the axles. Squeeze a small amount of lubricant onto each axle. Use your finger to gently spin each wheel several times to work the lubricant into the axles. Be careful not to knock the axles out of alignment. Your car is ready to race!

Materials & Tools

Materials:
- Official BSA Pinewood Derby Kit (available at craft and Scout stores)
- Tungsten weights (see Step 3 and pages 32–34; available at craft stores and online)
- Paint and/or decorations (see pages 22–27 for ideas)
- Dry graphite lubricant (available at craft and Scout stores)
- Masking tape: ¾" wide

- Sandpaper: 150 grit; wet/dry: 400, 600, and 1000 grit
- Newspaper or cardboard (see Step 8)
- Cyanoacrylate (CA) glue, such as Super Glue™
- Wood putty (optional, to fill holes; see page 34)
- Pipe cleaners (see page 41)
- Whitening toothpaste
- Paper towels

- Wheel spacer OR thin cardboard and tape to make one (see page 48)

Tools:
- Pencil
- Ruler
- Scissors
- Clamps
- Hand saw
- Paintbrushes (if needed)

- Digital scale
- Power drill or rotary tool and bits
- Triangular file OR glue sandpaper to craft sticks to make sanding sticks (see Step 14)
- Sharpie marker (to insert axles; see Step 22)
- Wheel mandrel (available at craft and Scout stores)

The author used these products for the project. Substitute your choice of brands, tools, and materials as desired.

Speed car flat pattern

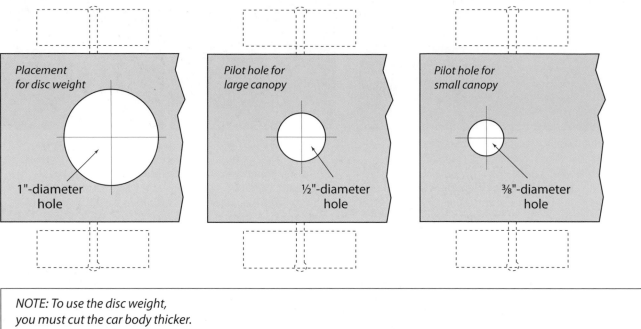

Placement for disc weight

1"-diameter hole

Pilot hole for large canopy

½"-diameter hole

Pilot hole for small canopy

⅜"-diameter hole

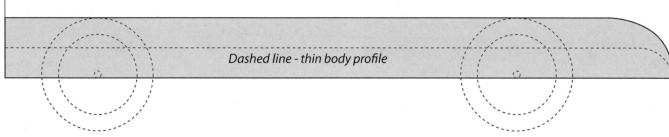

NOTE: To use the disc weight, you must cut the car body thicker.

Dashed line - thin body profile

Speed car wedge pattern

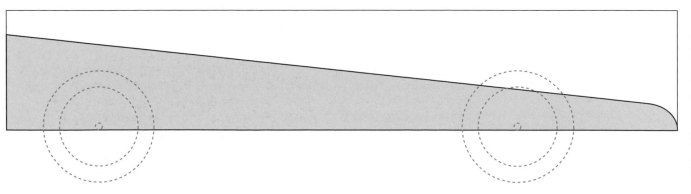

SHOP-TESTED CAR PATTERNS

While the flat and wedge-shaped cars on page 60 are proven winners, kids often want cars with more style. Here are 19 patterns to use, adapt, or inspire your designs. The axle locations and suggested weights are marked, but you should always weigh and balance your car to be sure it's tuned and ready to race.

- **Materials:** You can use the Official Pinewood Derby® Car Kit to make all of these designs. If you choose to use a block of pine wood instead, or you want to lengthen the wheelbase (see page 30), you'll need to drill holes for the axles using either a drill press or a hand-held drill and a tool such as the DerbyWorx Pro Body Tool or Pinewood Pro's Pro Driller™ Tool (see Resources, page 94).

- **Instructions:** You can follow the Basic Speed Car instructions (pages 54–59) to make all of these cars, referring to the detailed Speed Secrets on pages 29–53 as needed. However, some extra cutting may be required. After you cut the wood to the proper thickness for the designs on pages 63–68, you will need to use a coping saw or a scroll saw (pages 18–19) to make the decorative inside cuts in some of the patterns.

- **Compound Cutting:** Some of the cars on pages 69–80 will require compound cutting to achieve the shape. That means you will tape patterns to two sides of the block and cut the wood twice: first, cut the side view in as few cuts as possible; tape the waste wood back on to make a rectangle again; and then cut the top view and let the waste wood fall away. You may need to cut add-on pieces from the waste wood and glue them to the main car body using yellow wood glue and clamps (rubber bands might do in a pinch). See pages 82 and 89–90 for photos of compound cutting.

Recommended weights:

Thick slotted tungsten disc with tungsten cubes

THE DAYTONA
Designed by Derby Monkey

Recommended weights:

Tungsten cylinders

⅜"-diameter holes (9) for weights (optional)

Recommended weights:

Large tungsten canopy with tungsten cubes or putty

THE SPEEDSTER

Designed by Derby Monkey

Recommended weights:

Tungsten bars

Weight cover - 1/16" thick

LIGHTNING
Designed by Kristen Scanlan

Recommended weights:

Thick slotted tungsten disc with tungsten cubes or tungsten canopy

© 2016 Scroll Saw Woodworking & Crafts

THUNDER
Designed by Derby Monkey

Recommended weights:

Tungsten bars

Weight cover - ¹⁄₁₆" thick

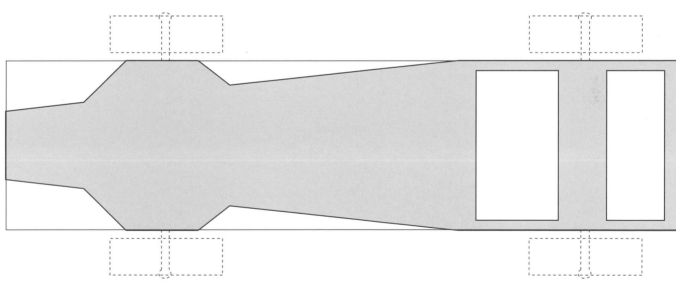

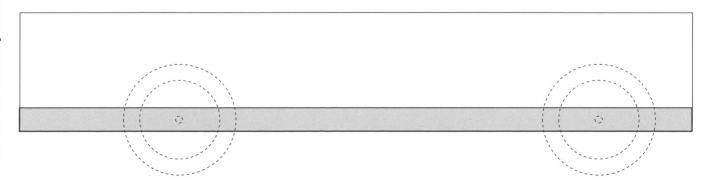

THE FLAME
Designed by Kristen Scanlan

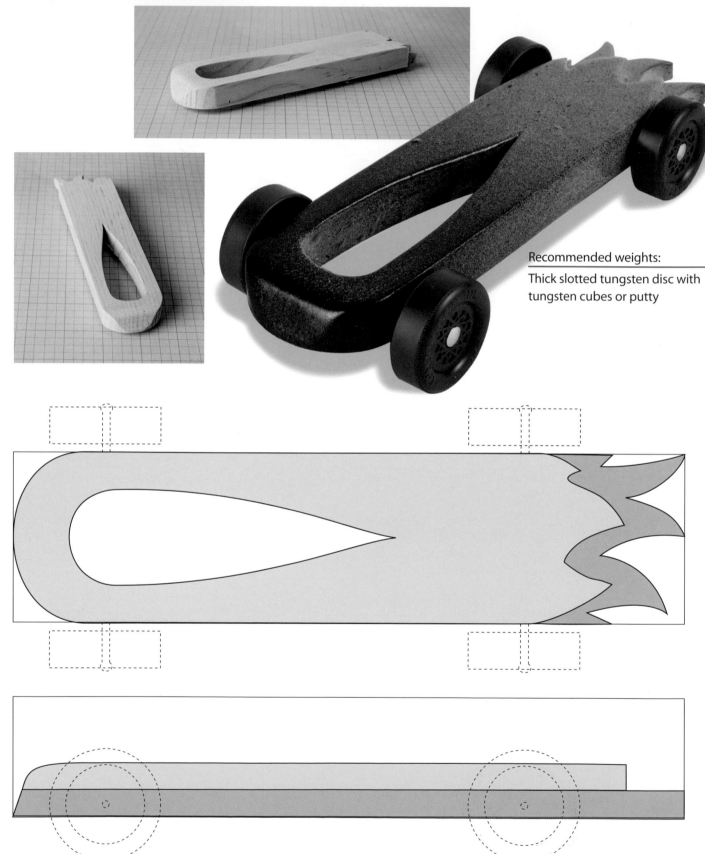

Recommended weights:

Thick slotted tungsten disc with tungsten cubes or putty

THE PHANTOM RACER
Designed by Derby Monkey

Recommended weights:

Tungsten bars

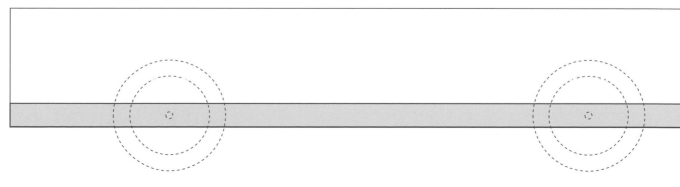

Weight cover - ¹⁄₁₆" thick

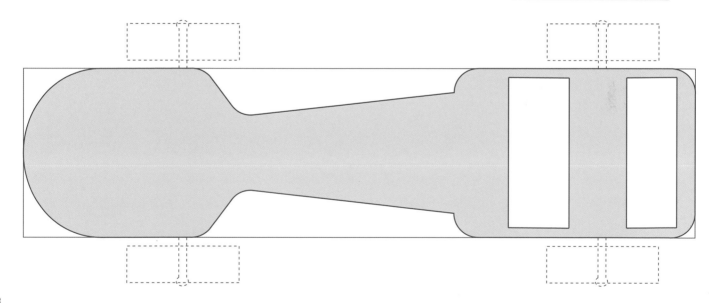

THE SKATEBOARD
Designed by Pinewood Pro

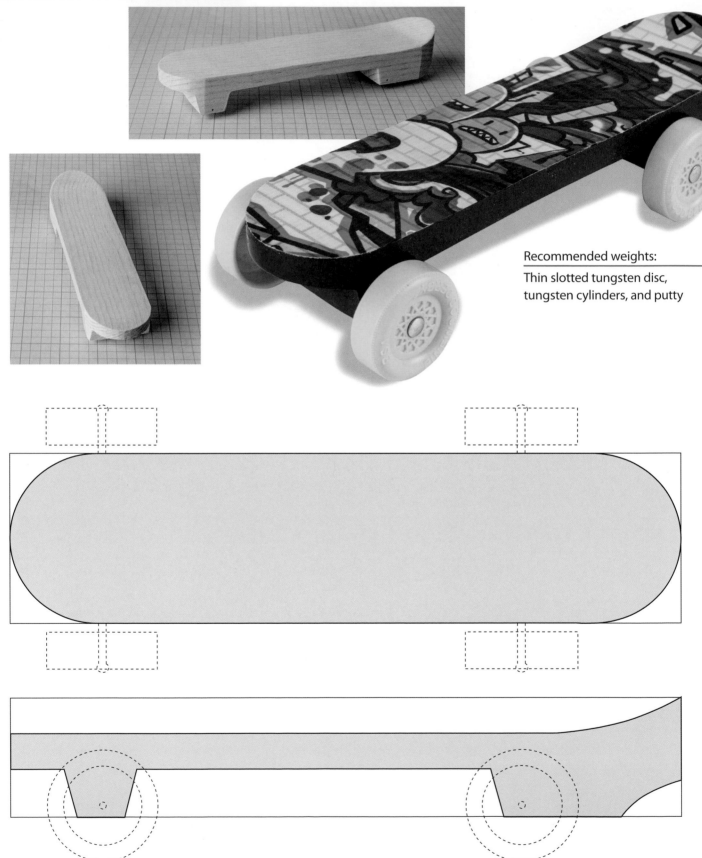

Recommended weights:

Thin slotted tungsten disc, tungsten cylinders, and putty

THE GRAND PRIX
Designed by Pinewood Pro

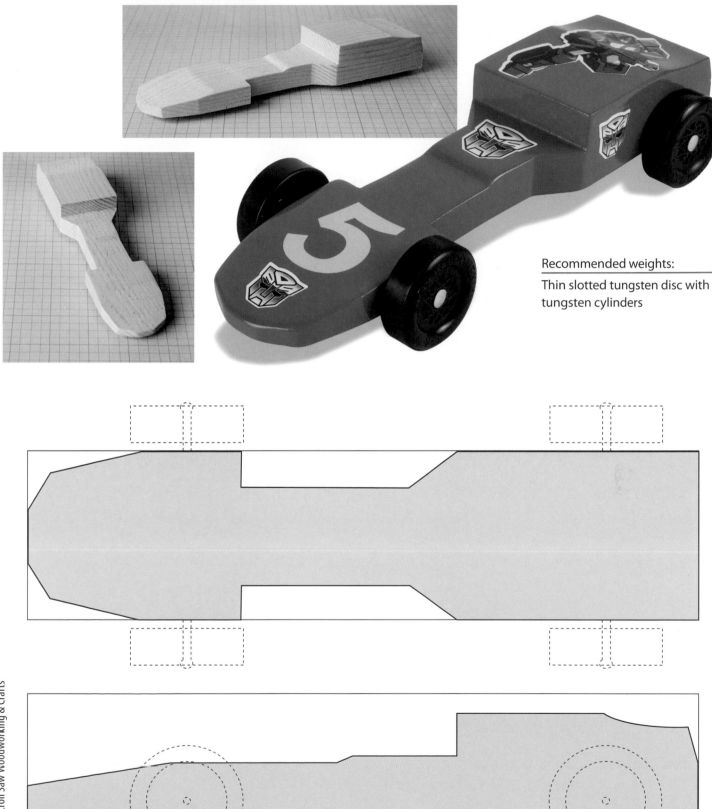

Recommended weights:

Thin slotted tungsten disc with tungsten cylinders

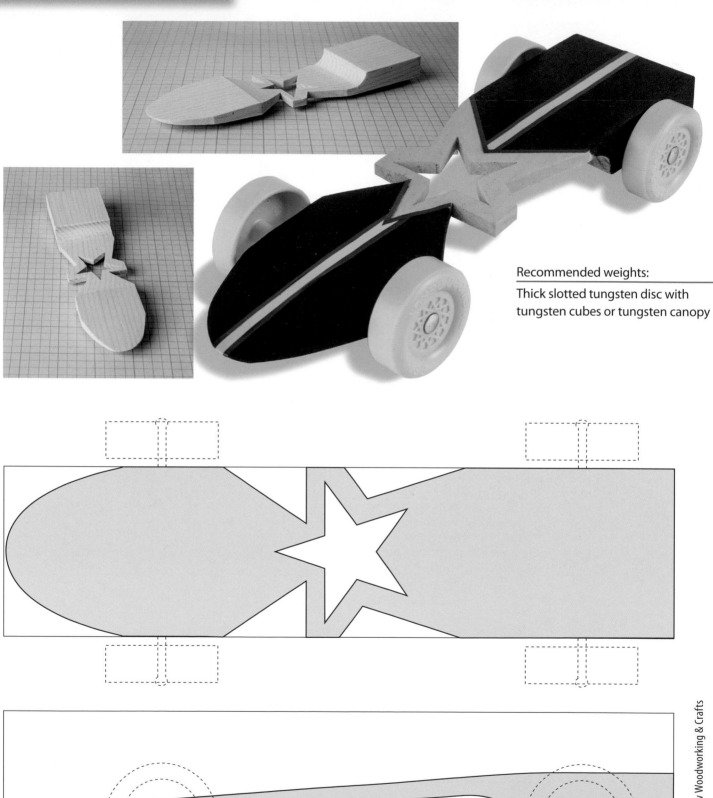

THE STAR
Designed by Sarah von Schmidt-Pauli

Recommended weights:

Thick slotted tungsten disc with tungsten cubes or tungsten canopy

© 2016 Scroll Saw Woodworking & Crafts

THE ARROW
Designed by Pinewood Pro

Recommended weights:

Thin slotted tungsten disc with tungsten cylinders

Recommended weights:

Thick slotted tungsten disc with tungsten cubes and putty or tungsten canopy

THE RIPPLE

Designed by Jon Deck

Recommended weights:

Large tungsten canopy

THE ROADSTER
Designed by Jon Deck

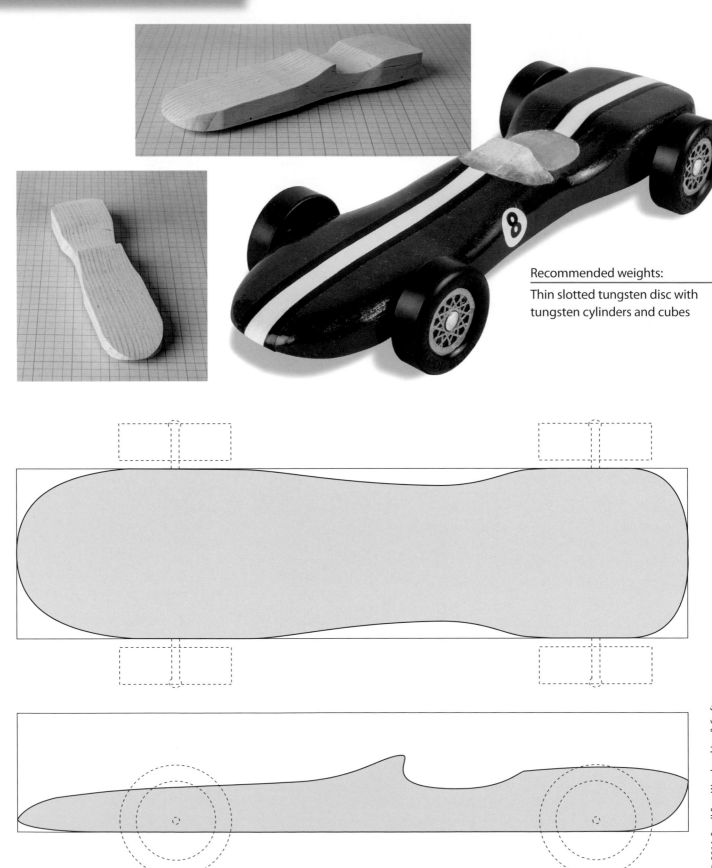

Recommended weights:

Thin slotted tungsten disc with tungsten cylinders and cubes

THE ASTRO
Designed by Llara Pazdan

Recommended weights:

Thin slotted tungsten disc with tungsten cylinders and cubes or putty

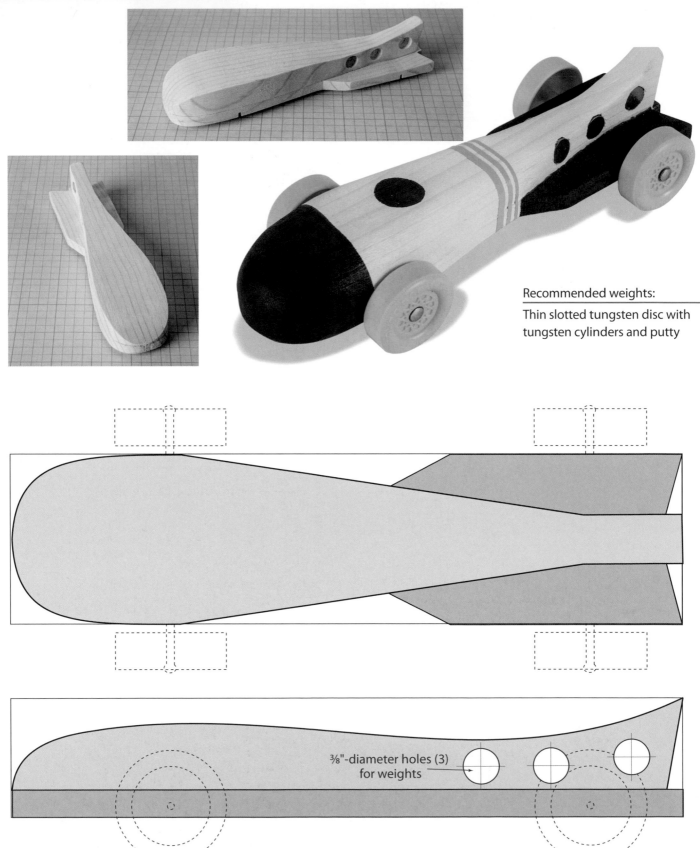

THE ROCKET
Designed by Kristen Scanlan

Recommended weights:

Thin slotted tungsten disc with tungsten cylinders and putty

⅜"-diameter holes (3) for weights

THE ORCA
Designed by Kristen Scanlan

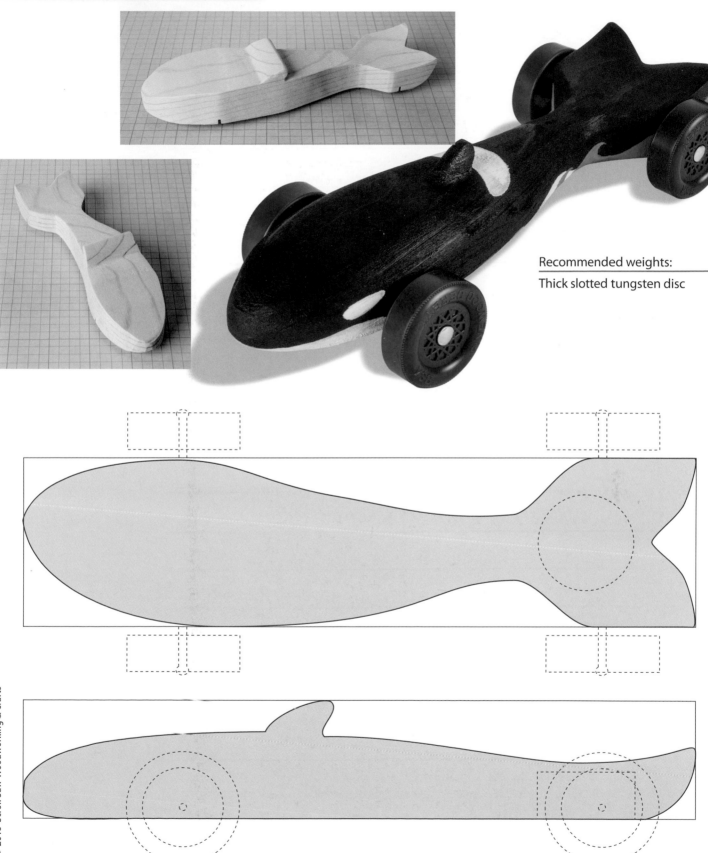

Recommended weights:

Thick slotted tungsten disc

THE STREAK
Designed by David Fisk

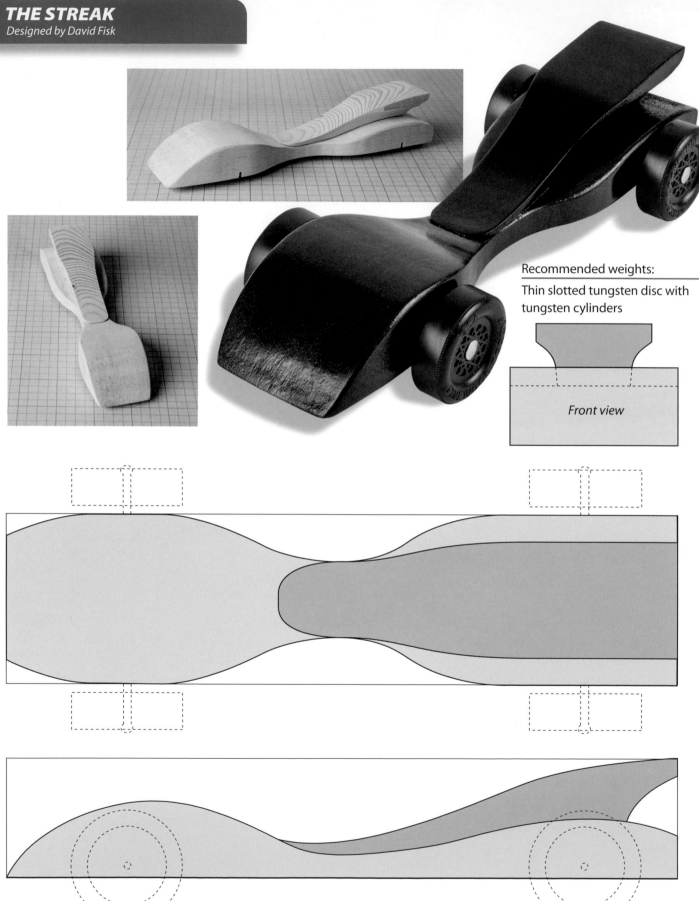

Recommended weights:

Thin slotted tungsten disc with tungsten cylinders

Front view

"DIESEL" DODGE CHARGER

A MUSCLE MACHINE POPULAR IN MOVIES, THIS CAR CAN INTIMIDATE OPPONENTS STANDING STILL

Designed by Jon Deck

The Dodge Charger is a hugely popular movie muscle car. Dominic Toretto's black 1970 R/T, with its super-charged 528ci Hemi bursting through the hood, dominates the *Fast & Furious* movie series. The Ghost Rider is driving a similar Charger on "Marvel's Agents of S.H.I.E.L.D." And, painted bright orange, the General Lee, a 1969 model, was as well known as the human stars of "The Dukes of Hazzard." This beauty is the personification of speed.

GETTING STARTED

You cannot build the Charger from the basic Pinewood Derby kit—you must purchase a larger piece of wood or glue together thinner wood. I used 1x4s to build mine. Either way, be sure the blocks are square by cutting them on a table saw. The body block is cut to 2" high by 2⅛" wide by 7¼" long. Cut two side blocks ½" wide by 1½" high by 7¼" long.

Cut the patterns along the rectangular perimeter lines for proper mounting.

1

Carefully attach the patterns to the wood. Use temporary-bond spray adhesive to attach the left body pattern to the narrow side of the block, aligning the pattern with the bottom of the wood. From the axle crosshairs, draw pencil lines across the bottom of the wood block using a square. Attach the axle position pattern on the opposite side of the block, aligning its axle crosshairs to the pencil lines and the pattern to the bottom of the wood. Attach the side patterns to their blocks. No special alignment is required for the sides.

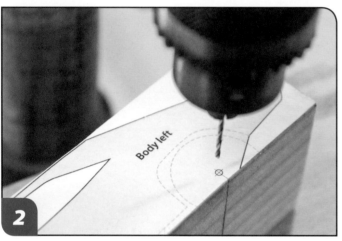

2

Drill the holes. Drill all four axle holes with a #44 bit as deep as possible. Use a drill press to ensure the axles are perpendicular to the body of the car.

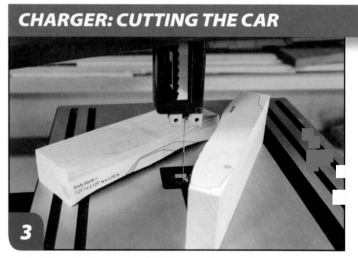

3

Cut the the blank in half. With a band saw, make one long cut along the body line to separate the roof from the body.

TIP

SAVE THE WASTE

Keep the top cutoff of the body blank. When it comes time to do any work on the underside of the car, the waste makes a perfect cradle to safely support your car. Be sure to pad the piece with a cloth, if your car has been painted.

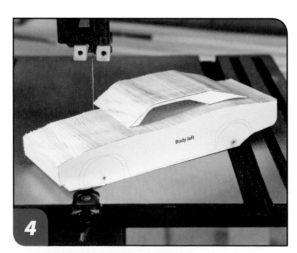

4

Cut the roof and body profiles. Use the band saw. First, carefully cut the inside profile of the roof. Then, cut its outside profile. Finish cutting the profile of the front and rear ends of the body of the car.

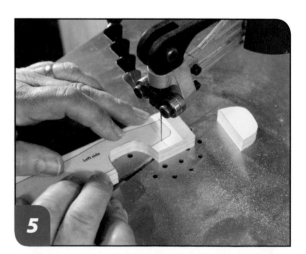

5

Cut the sides. Use a scroll saw to cut the right and left sides of the car. Be as precise as you can to minimize the shaping and sanding after the sides are attached to the body.

6

Join the sides to the body. Apply wood glue to the sides of the car. Carefully align them on the body before clamping them in place. Check the positioning of both sides after tightening the clamps to make sure they haven't slid out of alignment. Let the glue dry.

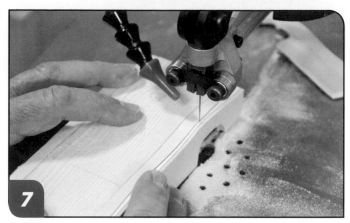

7

Cut the contoured sides. Cut the pattern for each side panel with a hobby knife from the top view pattern and attach them to the top of the car. Line the patterns up with the glue joint between the body and sides, being careful that the front and back are properly oriented. Cut the sides with the scroll saw.

CHARGER: SHAPING THE CAR

8

Sand the body and the roof. Remove the saw marks with a spindle, stationary belt, or pad sander. Sand all areas except where the roof joins the body. Sand the roof section as well, again avoiding the spots where the roof and body meet.

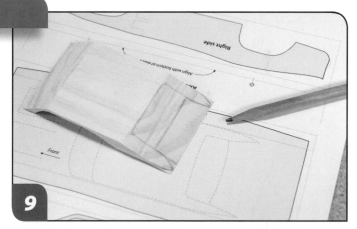

9

Mark the roof. Using a copy of the pattern, transfer the window and roof pillar lines onto the roof with a pencil. Cut the tails of roof pillars back to the edge of the rear window on the scroll saw. Cut along the bottom of the window to free the waste.

10

Shape the roof and body. Use a ½"-diameter sanding drum in a rotary tool, such as a Dremel, to soften the edges of the roof. Angle the sander to set in the rear window between the roof pillars. Shape the fenders, hood, trunk, and the front and rear ends of the body. Round the sides of the body near the bottom of the car.

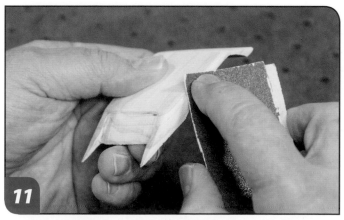

11

Finish sanding the car parts. Hand-sand the roof and body with progressively finer grits of sandpaper up to 220-grit. Remove all of the sanding marks left by the rotary tool. Again, avoid the areas where the body and roof will be joined.

12 Cut the front and rear recesses. Use a ⅛"-diameter cylinder-shaped rotary carving bit. For maximum control, hold the rotary tool against the workbench, and angle the carving tip to the proper height. Keep the tool stationary as you slide the car body back and forth to cut the top and bottom of the recess to the proper depth. Use a slight scrubbing motion to remove the remaining recessed area to the same depth.

13 Spot-paint the car. Use a small paintbrush to paint the interior of the car, inside of the roof, front and rear recesses, and the wheel wells with flat black paint. The flat finish will provide contrast with the high-gloss black on the rest of the car.

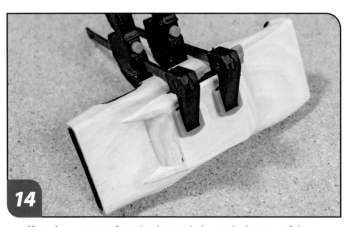

14 Glue the car together. Apply wood glue to the bottom of the windshield and the back portion of the roof that meets the body. Carefully align these pieces, front to back and side to side. Clamp the roof in place when properly aligned. Allow the glue to set.

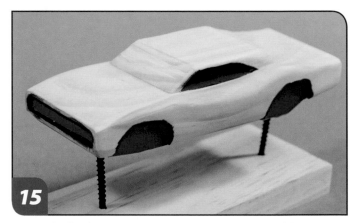

15 Do the final painting prep. Check the glue joint and fill any gaps with a lightweight spackle. Smooth the joint with your finger, and lightly sand the spackle when dry with 220-grit sandpaper. Mask the areas of flat black with painter's tape. Mount the car on a stand made from a block of wood and long drywall screws.

CHARGER: PAINTING THE CAR

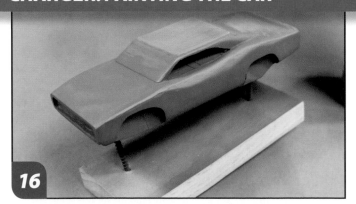

16 Apply the primer coat. Apply several light coats of a sandable primer. When dry, lightly hand-sand the finish with 400-grit wet-dry sandpaper. This will fill minor imperfections and provide a smooth surface for the finish coat.

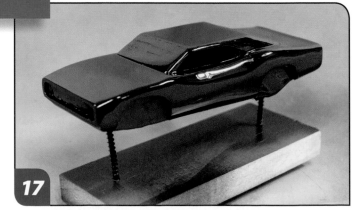

17 Paint the car. Spray several light coats of gloss black onto the car. Allow the recommended dry time between coats. Be patient. Each coat will build to achieve a smooth finish. Let the car dry overnight before handling it.

18

19

Print and apply stickers. Scan the window, grill, and rear end sticker art to your computer or download the art from our website (www.scrollsawer.com). Print the art onto self-adhesive label paper available at office supply stores. Apply several coats of a high gloss clear spray finish. Cut out the sticker art with a hobby knife when dry. Apply the windshield and rear window. The grill and rear end stickers fit into the recesses of the car.

Cut the engine. The engine is built from two small pieces cut from waste wood: one for the block, and one for the fuel injector air intake. The defining details of the engine are the three intake ports. I cut them with a ⅛"-diameter cylinder-shaped rotary carving bit. Draw the outline of the intake on the end a larger piece of ³⁄₁₆"-thick wood. Hold the rotary tool in one position while you move the wood into the bit. Cut the middle hole first, and then cut the other two. Finally, cut the perimeter of the intake and engine block pieces on the scroll saw.

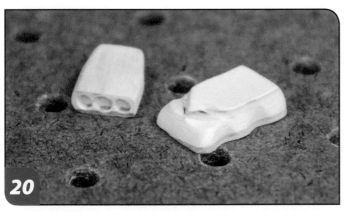

20

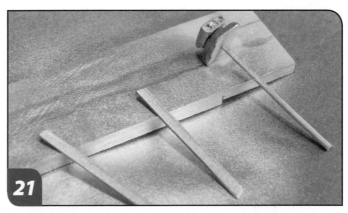

21

Shape the engine. Round and taper the edges of the air intake with a ¼"-diameter sanding drum in the Dremel. Bevel the edges of the engine block and round in some small details. Create a scalloped edge on the left and right of the block. When you're satisfied with the shape, hand-sand it with 220-grit sandpaper. Glue the engine parts together with wood glue.

Finish the add-ons. Cut the two bumpers and sand them smooth. Paint the engine and bumpers with metallic silver paint. Mount the engine on a bamboo skewer to hold it while painting. When dry, use the end of the skewer to dot red paint in the three intake ports. Mount the engine and bumpers to the car with cyanoacrylate (CA) glue. Attach tuned wheels, adjust the weight, and lubricate the car.

Materials & Tools

Wood:
Cut the following blocks from pine or basswood:
- Body: 2" x 2⅛" x 7¼"
- Sides, 2 each: ½" x 1½" x 7¼"
- Bumpers, 2 each: ⅛" x ¼" x 3"

Materials:
- Spray adhesive: temporary-bond
- Sandpaper: 150, 220, 400 wet/dry
- Glue: wood; cyanoacrylate (CA)
- Lightweight spackling

- Scrap wood and drywall screws (painting platform)
- Primer: sandable spray
- Spray enamel: high gloss black, metallic silver
- Paint, acrylic: flat black, red
- Peel and stick label: white coated
- Spray clear finish: gloss
- Permanent marker, such as Sharpie: silver (wheel spokes)
- Bamboo skewer

- Official BSA wheels and axles: 4 each, race-tuned
- Car weights

Tools:
- Saws: table, band, scroll
- Scroll saw blades: #5 skip-tooth
- Pencil
- Small square
- Drill press with #44 bit
- Sanders: stationary belt, spindle, or pad

- Rotary tool, such as Dremel brand, with bits: ¼", ½"-dia. sanding drum, ⅛"-dia. cylinder-shaped high-speed steel cutter
- Paintbrushes
- Computer and ink-jet printer
- Small clamps
- Hobby knife

The author used these products for the project. Substitute your choice of brands, tools, and materials as desired.

NOTE *If the finished car weighs more than 5.0 ounces, use a large Forstner bit to drill holes in the underside of the car near the front. Add tungsten plates or putty at the back as necessary to properly weight and balance the car.*

Charger patterns

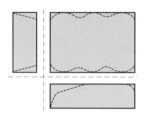

Air intake
³⁄₁₆" x ½" x ⅝"

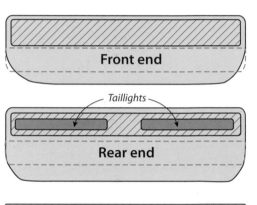

Engine block
¼" x ⅝" x ⅞"

Front end

Taillights

Rear end

Bumper - Cut 2

Charger stickers
Photcopy onto sticker paper.

Front grill

Back end

Front windshield

Back window

Charger patterns

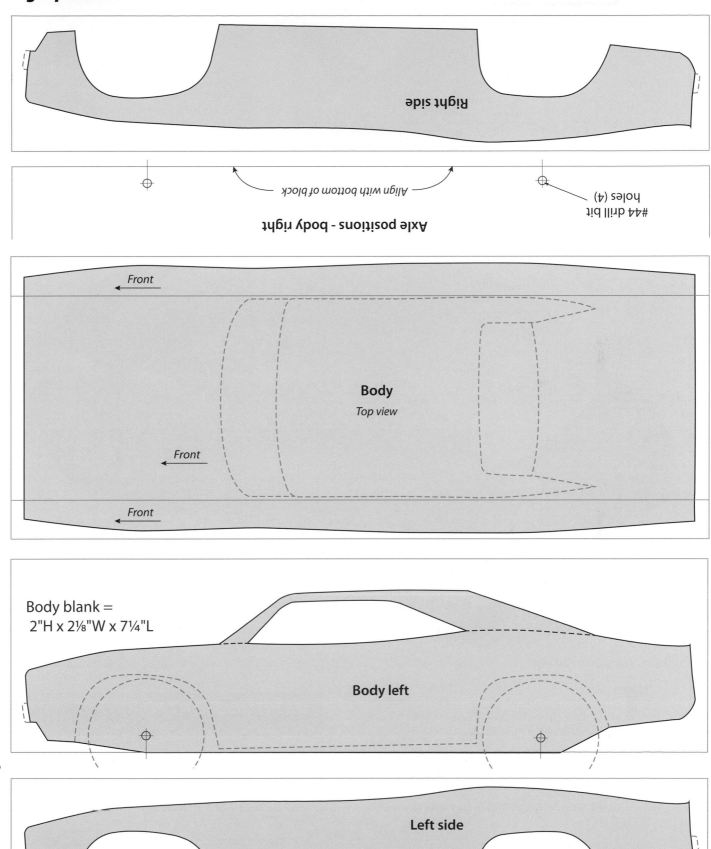

Right side

Axle positions - body right

Align with bottom of block

#44 drill bit
holes (4)

Body
Top view

Front

Front

Front

Body blank =
2"H x 2⅛"W x 7¼"L

Body left

Left side

Side blanks =
½"W x 1½"H x 7¼"L

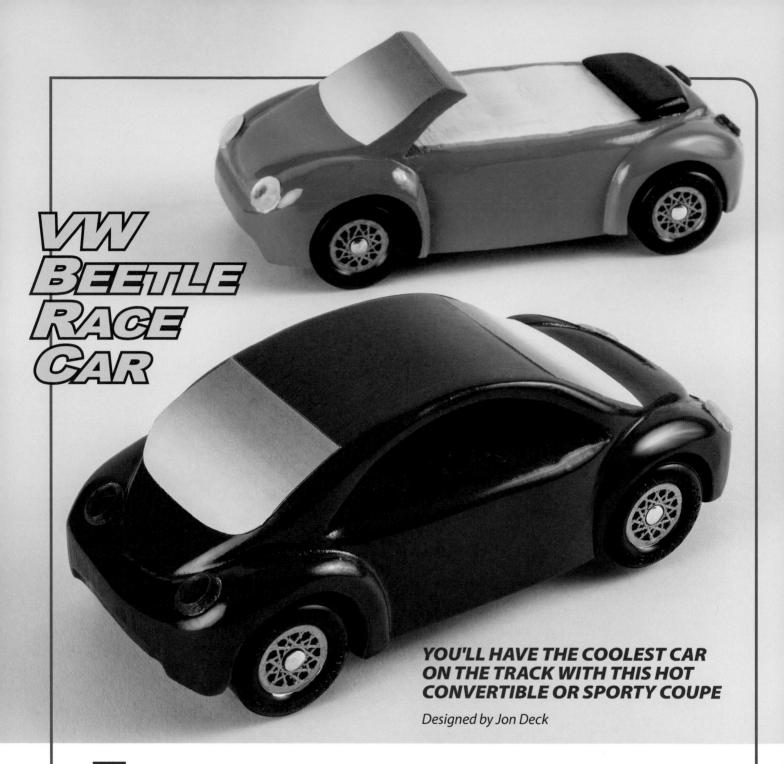

VW BEETLE RACE CAR

YOU'LL HAVE THE COOLEST CAR ON THE TRACK WITH THIS HOT CONVERTIBLE OR SPORTY COUPE

Designed by Jon Deck

The original Volkswagen Beetle—the Bug—is one of the most famous cars on the planet, with something like 21 million built over 70 years. So it's no surprise that the redesigned Beetle, which was introduced in 1998, has been crazy popular, too. Our version will be a fun contender at your Derby.

You'll need to cut and glue together several pieces to form the car's body. Then, sand carefully to produce a faithful reproduction of the Beetle ready to paint, tune up, and race.

GETTING STARTED

You cannot build this car from the basic Pinewood Derby kit. Purchase larger wood or glue together thinner wood. I used 1x4s to build mine. Either way, be sure it's square by cutting it on a table saw. Cut the block to 2⅜" high by 3" wide by 7" long.

Likewise, cut the patterns along the rectangular perimeters for proper mounting.

1

Carefully attach the patterns to the wood. Use temporary-bond spray adhesive to attach the left body pattern to the narrow side of the block, aligning the pattern with the bottom of the block. From the axle crosshairs, draw pencil lines across the bottom of the wood using a square. Attach the axle position pattern on the opposite side of the block, aligning its axle crosshairs to the pencil lines and the pattern to the bottom of the block. Also mark the bottom with 9⁄16" depth marks for boring the wheel wells.

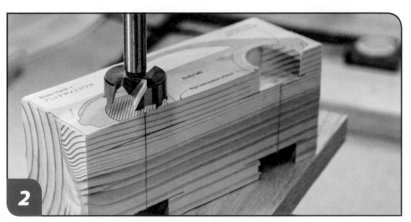

2

Drill the holes. Drill all four axle holes with a #44 bit as deep as possible. Use a drill press to ensure the axles are perpendicular to the body of the car. On the drill press, bore the wheel wells with a 1⅜"-diameter Forstner bit using the axle holes for center. Bore to the 9⁄16" pencil marks on the bottom of the blank.

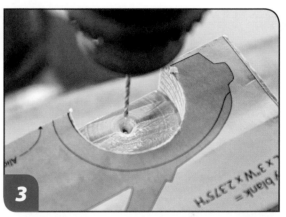

3

Redrill the axle holes. Return the #44 bit to the drill press and deepen all of the axle holes as far as you can.

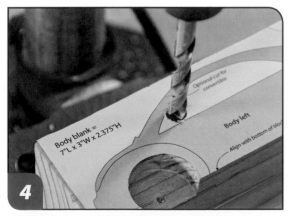

4

Drill a hole in the window area. Chuck a ⅜"-diameter bit in the drill press, and drill a hole through the window area of the body. This will allow you to freely move the car around as you make the interior cut on the band saw.

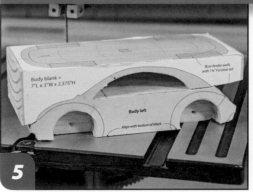

5

Cut the side profile. With the band saw, cut the interior window first. Begin at the back of the car and cut along the lower part of the window to the pivoting hole. Rotate the car, and cut the top of the window opening. Turn the saw off and back the blade out of the cut to remove the waste. Re-enter the cutout and trim out the notch at the front of the window. Cut the front and back bumper details next. If you're making the convertible, cut the dashed line at the top of the windshield.

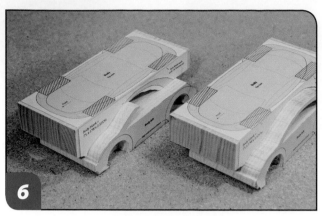

6

Finish the side profile cut. Cut the remaining outline of the car. For the convertible, do not cut along the roofline to the back of the car. This will ensure that the waste portion can be secured tightly to the car when you make the top profile cuts.

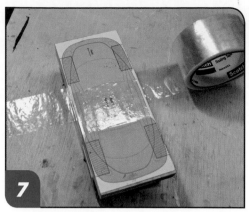

7

Attach the top waste piece. Making sure the alignment of the two pieces is correct, wrap the two securely with clear packing tape.

BEETLE: MAKING THE COMPOUND CUT

8

Cut the outside top profile. Remove the section between the fenders on both sides of the car first. Then, cut the front and back of the car. Make sure you're not cutting all the tape off the sides of the blank assembly. The two pieces must stay in perfect alignment for an accurate fit after cutting.

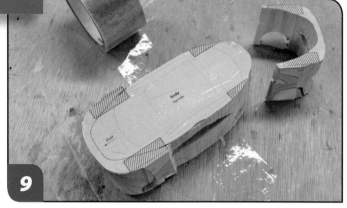

9

Cut the front and rear sections. Rewrap the blank assembly with tape before cutting the front and rear sections of the car. After freeing the front section, secure that side with tape again to prevent any shifting between the pieces while you cut the rear section. Remove all of the patterns after you complete the cutting.

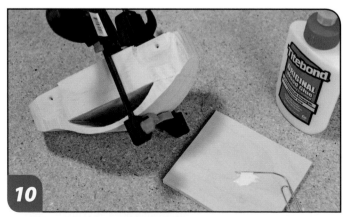

10

Rejoin the back of the roof. With a paper clip, work some wood glue in the kerf between the body and the roof. Tighten the joint with a small clamp. Set aside until the glue is dry.

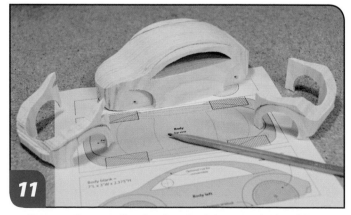

11

Prepare the parts for shaping. Sand the top and sides of the body on a stationary belt sander to remove the saw marks. Do not sand in the areas where the fender sections will mate with the body. Using the patterns, sketch the shaping lines onto the parts.

BEETLE: SHAPING THE CAR

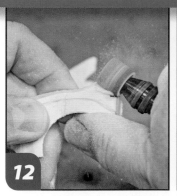

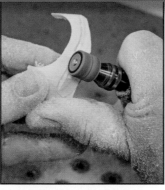

12

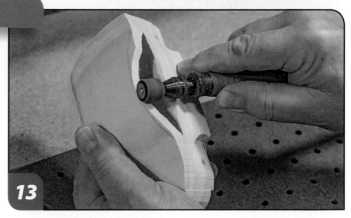

13

Shape the fender sections. You can perform all the rough shaping with a ½"-diameter sanding drum chucked into a rotary tool, such as a Dremel. Shape the areas where you need to remove the most wood first to achieve the basic shape. Then, round the fenders and bumpers. Be careful when handling the fender sections because the ends are fragile and could break off.

Shape the body. Use the rotary tool and ½"-diameter sanding drum to remove the curved section on both sides of the roof. Dry-fit the shaped fender sections and trace their outlines onto the body with a pencil. Round the hood and trunk edges of the car, but do not shape where the fenders will attach to the body.

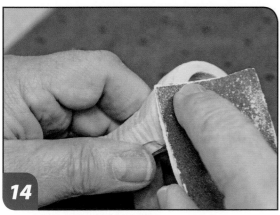

14

15

Join the parts of the car. Use a construction adhesive, such as Liquid Nails for Projects, to attach the fender sections to the body. The thick adhesive not only glues the parts together, it fills in the gaps between. Secure the parts with painter's tape at the bumpers and a small clamp at the ends of the fenders. *NOTE: Check the alignment of parts carefully before and after clamping.* Allow 24 hours to cure. Fill in any remaining gaps in the car with a lightweight spackle before painting.

Finish-sand the parts of the car. Hand-sand all non-joining areas of the body and the fender sections with progressively finer grits of sandpaper to up 220-grit. Smooth all of the sanding lines left by the rotary tool. Again, be careful with the ends of the fenders.

BEETLE: PAINTING THE CAR

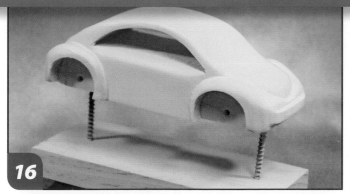

16

17

Apply a primer coat to the car. Fashion a stand out of a small block of wood and a couple of long drywall screws. Mount the car by driving the screws into the bottom of the car. Paint the car with a few coats of sandable primer. Allow it to dry.

Paint the finish coat. Sand the primer with 400-grit wet-dry sandpaper. Apply several coats of spray paint and allow the recommended dry time between coats. Let the paint dry completely.

Print and apply stickers. Apply several coats of a high gloss clear spray finish and let dry. Scan the window sticker art to your computer or download the art from our website (www. scrollsawer.com). Print the art onto self-adhesive label paper available at office supply stores. Cut out the window art with a hobby knife and apply it to the car.

Make headlights and taillights. Sand the faceted surfaces of clear and red 20mm-diameter craft jewels until the jewels are slightly rounded. Sand off the edges with a rotary sanding wheel to form a ½" by ⅜" oval shape. Spray the jewels with a high-gloss clear finish. Mark the light positions on the front and rear of the car. Carefully sand a flat area for the jewels, if necessary. Attach them with cyanoacrylate (CA) glue.

Make a tonneau cover (convertible only). Apply the pattern to a ³⁄₁₆"-thick piece of wood and cut it with a scroll saw. Sand the tonneau cover. Paint the interior area of the car and the tonneau cover a color of your choice, let dry, and glue the cover in place. Attach tuned wheels, adjust the weight, and lubricate the car.

NOTE *If you find that the finished car weighs more than 5.0 ounces, use a large Forstner bit to drill holes in the underside near the front. Add tungsten plates or putty at the back as necessary to properly weight and balance the car.*

Materials & Tools

Materials:
- Pine or basswood: body, 2⅜" x 3" x 7"
- Pine or basswood: tonneau cover (convertible only), ³⁄₁₆" x ⅞" x 2"
- Spray adhesive: temporary-bond
- Tape: clear packaging, blue painter's
- Sandpaper: assorted grits from 100 to 400
- Paper clip
- Glue: wood, cyanoacrylate (CA)
- Construction adhesive, such as Liquid Nails for Projects
- Spackle
- Scrap wood and drywall screws (painting platform)
- Sandable primer
- Spray enamel: colors of choice
- Self-adhesive ink-jet label paper
- Spray clear finish: gloss
- Permanent marker, such as Sharpie: silver (wheel spokes)

- Craft jewels, 20mm round: headlights, 2 each clear; taillights, 2 each red
- Official BSA wheels and axles: 4 each race-tuned
- Car weights of choice

Tools:
- Saws: table, band, scroll (convertible only)
- Scroll saw blades: #5 skip-tooth (convertible only)
- Pencil
- Ruler
- Small square
- Drill press with bits: #44, ⅜"-dia. twist; 1⅜"-dia. Forstner
- Stationary belt sander
- Small clamp
- Rotary tool, such as Dremel, with ½"-dia. sanding drum
- Paintbrush
- Computer and ink-jet printer
- Hobby knife

The author used these products for the project. Substitute your choice of brands, tools, and materials as desired.

Windshield stickers
Photcopy onto sticker paper.

Front

Rear

VW Beetle patterns

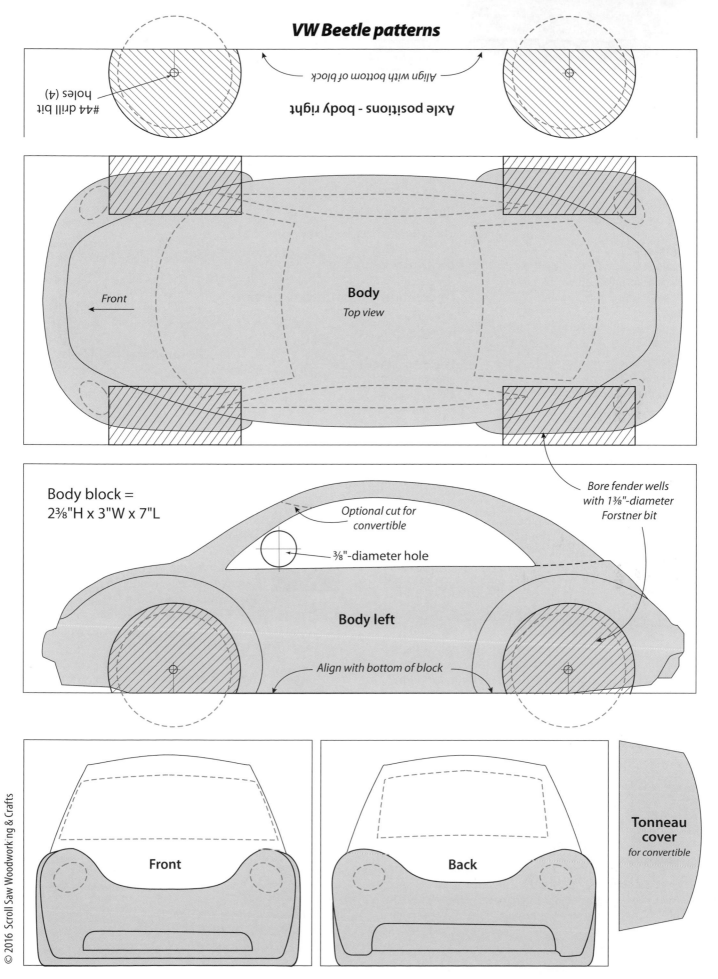

Axle positions - body right

#44 drill bit holes (4).

Align with bottom of block

Body
Top view

Front

Bore fender wells with 1⅜"-diameter Forstner bit

Body block = 2⅜"H x 3"W x 7"L

Optional cut for convertible

⅜"-diameter hole

Body left

Align with bottom of block

Front

Back

Tonneau cover
for convertible

RESOURCES

Official Pinewood Derby Supplies & Alignment Tools

Boy Scouts of America
800-323-0736
www.scoutstuff.org

Derby Monkey
888-286-8920
www.derbymonkey.com

DerbyWorx
www.derbyworx.com

Pinewood Pro
203-400-3713
www.pinewoodpro.com

Revell, Inc.
847-758-3200
www.revell.com

Car Designs & Tips

Lowes/Dremel Dremel Derby
1-800-4-DREMEL
www.dremelderby.com

Decorations: Tape, Stickers, Paint

A.C. Moore
www.acmoore.com

Duck® Brand Duct Tape
800-321-0253
www.duckbrand.com

Hobby Lobby
www.hobbylobby.com

Jo-Ann Fabric and Crafts
www.joann.com

Michaels
www.michaels.com

The Testor Corp.
800-837-8677 (800-TESTORS)
www.testors.com

Rotary/Shaping Tools

Dremel
800-437-3635
www.dremel.com

CONTRIBUTORS

Jon Deck
Jon Deck is the magazine art director at Fox Chapel Publishing. A former Boy Scout and Scout leader, Jon has been a woodworker and hobbyist for most of his adult life. You can reach him at Jon@FoxChapelPublishing.com.

Joe Gargiulo of Pinewood Pro
Joe Gargiulo is the owner of Pinewood Pro, an online Pinewood Derby supply store. A professional engineer, former Scout, and Scouting parent, Joe has written a number of booklets about racing, including *Winning Pinewood Derby Secrets* and *Pinewood Derby in Six Steps*. He has also designed his own tools to help make winning cars. Visit his website at www.PinewoodPro.com.

David Meade
The author of the best-selling book *Pinewood Derby Speed Secrets*, David Meade got his start in the Pinewood Derby as a boy, when his family was well known for building unbeatable cars. His sons carried on the winning tradition by garnering 13 first-place championships over seven consecutive years. By profession, David is a research scientist. His background in research and experimental design enabled him to develop a unique and powerful approach to Pinewood Derby racing. He also enjoys model rocketry and astronomy.

Steve Robbins
Steve Robbins is the owner of Derby Monkey, an online Pinewood Derby supply store. He also serves as the department chair and a professor for the Tyler Junior College Vision Care Technology program in Tyler, Texas. Steve is a previous Scout Master and has accumulated years of experience in developing and testing Pinewood Derby car speed techniques. Visit his website at www.DerbyMonkey.com.

Troy Thorne
A designer and woodworker, Troy Thorne participated in Scouting activities with his son, Nathan, for many years. He drew on his artistic roots and personal experience, as well as the experiences of other top Derby car designers, to create several best-selling books, including Pinewood *Derby Designs & Patterns, Getting Started in Pinewood Derby,* and *Building the Fastest Pinewood Derby Car* (all available from Fox Chapel Publishing). Troy also uses his skills for large-scale projects—he has built a street-legal AC Cobra replica, furniture, and canoes.

Special thanks to the Fox Design Team, who provided some of our car patterns: David Fisk, Llara Pazdan, Kristen Scanlan, and Sarah von Schmidt-Pauli.

INDEX

INDEX